Macroeconomics

Macroeconomics

Big Things Have Small Beginnings

FIRST EDITION

Giacomo Santangelo, Ph.D.

Fordham University & Stillman School of Business, Seton Hall University

cognella®

SAN DIEGO

Bassim Hamadeh, CEO and Publisher
Mary Jane Peluso, Senior Specialist Acquisitions Editor
Alisa Munoz, Project Editor
Casey Hands, Associate Production Editor
Emely Villavicencio, Senior Graphic Designer
Greg Isales, Licensing Associate
Natalie Piccotti, Director of Marketing
Kassie Graves, Vice President of Editorial
Jamie Giganti, Director of Academic Publishing

Cover image: Copyright © 2019 iStockphoto LP/normaals.

Printed in the United States of America.

3970 Sorrento Valley Blvd., Ste. 500, San Diego, CA 92121

For Carmen.

All at once, everything is different . . .

Contents

Preface

It's time to play the music
It's time to light the lights...

Jim Henson

In my experience, when it comes to study *economics*, students fall into three distinct categories: students who took Econ in high school and *love it*, those who took it in high school and *hate it,* and those who have no formal training in economics, whatsoever. Regardless of which of these three groups a student falls into, as an educator, *my* job is to bring light to a topic that is at once *as old as time* yet, possessing endless *new horizons to pursue*. Economics is so much more than the study of scarcity.

When I was an undergraduate, I realized that there are two kinds of economics: the kind that is discussed in the news, due to its far-reaching effect on society (which happens to be the topic of this text,) and the kind that directly affects the individual. If one reads of high levels of unemployment, one may be concerned. If one *becomes* unemployed, one may be devastated. Not long after taking-up the study of economics, I realized that despite the dual nature of economics, at its core, those two studies inform one another. To quote T. E. Lawrence, "Big things have small beginnings."

With this text, I hope to address the economic issues that students will be faced-with in the media (both traditional and social,) paying specific attention to the interconnectedness of all things *economics*. One must realize that the enigma that lies at the heart of the inner machinations of the individual economic agent and the maximization of aggregate social benefit are not mutually exclusive.

At the end of every chapter, I have included "Food for Thought". These, hopefully, non-threatening questions, call upon the student to *think* about the material in the chapter, in some way external to the text. Whether that means finding more current data or finding a current example, in the news, it is my hope that students will come to *see* the subject matter, everywhere.

I wish to extend my thanks to Cognella for giving me this opportunity, especially, Mary Jane Peluso, Senior Acquisitions Editor, who talked me into writing this text; Emely Villavicencio, senior graphic designer, for my cover; my wonderfully patient project editor, Alisa Muñoz; and my understanding associate production editor, Casey Hands.

This book would not have been possible if not for the *many* professors with whom I have had the honor to work over the course of the years that I have studied and worked, in the field. There are literally too many to list; however, I would be remiss, if I did not express my appreciation for the benefit that I have enjoyed from knowing, studying with, and teaching alongside professors like Henry Amoroso, Mary Burke, Kristine Kintanar, Darryl McLeod, and Angela Weisel.

I cannot, in all honesty, begin to express my continuing gratitude to Professors Dominick Salvatore, Henry Schwalbenberg, and, most importantly, Derrick Reagle. The guidance that you provided me *literally* enabled me to write this book. Thank you.

Chapter 1

Introduction to Macroeconomics

> A beginning is the time for taking
> the most delicate care that the
> balances are correct.
>
> Frank Herbert

It would seem that *every* chapter 1 in *every* economics textbook allocates a great deal of time to differentiating between *micro* and *macro*economics. Suffice it to say that, once you know that economics is the study of how various *agents*[1] behave in the face of scarcity, it allows us the ability to *jump right in.*

We can define **microeconomics** as the study of how individual consumers (like the reader) and individual firms (like the publisher of this text) make decisions in the face of uncertainty.[2] Asking how we, individually, experience the economy, we can break the study of micro into four topics:

- Demand and supply theory
- Consumer behavior theory
- Production theory
- Market behavior theory

Macroeconomics has traditionally concerned itself, not with the individual, but with the nation as a whole. Instead of the publisher of this book, we discuss

---

[1] Consumers, firms, governments

[2] How to best allocate time, money, energy, labor, capital, etc.,

the producers of *all goods and services* in the country. Instead of looking to the individual reader of the book, we speak of *all consumers* in the country. Macroeconomics, then, speaks to the *overall* economic experience of the country. We can break the study of macro down into four topics, as well:

- Inflation
- Unemployment
- Business cycles
- Long run growth

Where a microeconomist might ask how the book's publisher will likely be affected by the introduction of a technology that makes its labor force better, faster, and stronger, or how an individual consumer may be affected by the loss of her job, macroeconomists are concerned with how the overall production possibilities of the national economy are affected by a more dynamically efficient labor force, or what effect increases in unemployment have on the general economic well-being of the nation.

1.1   A Taste of Macroeconomics

As stated earlier, macroeconomics is about issues much larger than the individual. These issues include topics like inflation, unemployment, and long run economic growth (all of which will be discussed in more detail, in later chapters.) We will now look at some data from the Federal Reserve Bank of St. Louis to get an idea of how economists use time-series analysis to examine the macroeconomy.

- Inflation

Inflation is defined as the general increase in price levels. There are several common measures of inflation that we will cover later on, one of which is the *Consumer Price Index,* which measures changes in the price of consumer goods, purchased by the typical household.

It is common for economic data scientists to identify *recession years* with shaded areas, on graphs. In figure 1.1, we see an inverse relationship between these recession years and consumer prices. (Price levels tend to *fall* during recessions.)

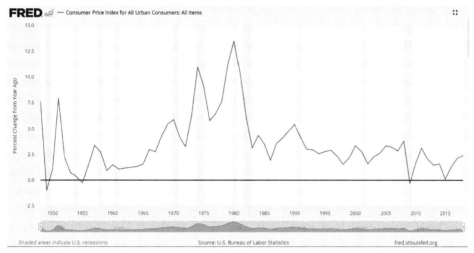

Figure 1.1 Index of change in US consumer prices, 1948–2018

■ Unemployment

When looking at the overall health of the labor market, the most widely accepted measure of joblessness is the *Civilian Unemployment Rate* or *U3*. It is, simply, the proportion of the labor force who are without a job and who are actively seeking work. Notice, in recession years, *U3* increases.[3]

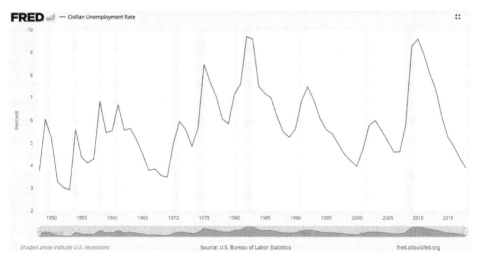

Figure 1.2 US civilian unemployment, 1948–2018

---

[3]In chapter 3, we will have a more in-depth discussion of unemployment.

■ Long-Run Economic Growth

For reasons that we will discuss later, many economists measure the overall economic well-being of a nation using *per-capita real gross domestic product (GDP)*. We arrive at per-capita real GDP by dividing the dollar value of all domestic economic activity in the economy, by the population, giving us, roughly, the economic benefit enjoyed by the average person in the nation. To this end, economists use the change in per-capita GDP as a measure of *economic growth.*

Figure 1.3 shows 70 years of US economic growth, as reflected by increasing per-capita real GDP.

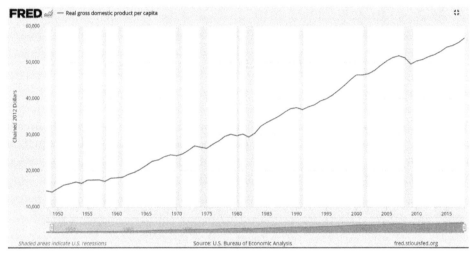

Figure 1.3 US per-capita real GDP, 1948–2018

1.2 Macroeconomics at Work

Macroeconomists analyze data in the hope of identifying trends and cycles this allows them to forecast future conditions of the economy. For example, it would not be surprising to find a macroeconomist analyzing global financial data that might predict the next financial crisis, similar to the one that affected global markets in 2008.

Macroeconomists can be found, mainly, in three areas:

1. Academia
   The *Oxford English Dictionary* defines an academic as "a member of a uni-

versity or college's teaching or research staff."[4] Academic economists are easy to find. It is likely that the person who *instructed* you to purchase this book is an academic. Academic economists are charged with teaching the future generations the *mysteries* of markets and trends.

2. Government
When you are listening to the morning news, ever wonder where the unemployment or inflation numbers come from? When the president of the United States announces new economic policy meant to *stimulate* a lagging economy, ever wonder who advises him on that? Whether it is an analyst at the *Bureau of Labor Statistics*,[5] a researcher at the the *St. Louis Federal Reserve Bank*,[6] or a member of the *Council of Economic Advisors*,[7] Macroeconomists play an integral role in the view and shape of the economy.

3. The private sector
Whether it is building macroeconomic models to predict future global market conditions for an investment bank, developing new techniques to address quantitative problems and contribute to the design of automated systems at an international health insurance company, or serving as an advisor to an international labor organization, macroeconomists are *key* to collecting, analyzing, and advising in the world of global business.

For more information on jobs for economists, please visit the Job Openings for Economists website, run by the American Economic Association.[8]

1.3 Select Macroeconomic Blogs

Ever wonder what macroeconomists think about, when they aren't at work?

- http://gregmankiw.blogspot.com/
- https://marginalrevolution.com/
- https://delong.typepad.com/
- https://johnhcochrane.blogspot.com/
- https://giacomosantangelo.blogspot.com/

---

[4]"academic, n.". OED Online. March 2019. Oxford University Press. https://www.oed.com/view/Entry/880?redirectedFrom=academic
[5]Bureau of Labor Statistics, https://www.bls.gov/
[6]St. Louis Federal Reserve Bank, https://fred.stlouisfed.org/
[7]Council of Economic Advisors, https://www.whitehouse.gov/cea/
[8]"JOE Network," American Economic Association, https://www.aeaweb.org/joe/

Food for Thought

1. In the news, over the last week, find five articles/stories in which an economist was involved/quoted. List and explain the economist's role, in the article.

2. Go to the Job Openings for Economists website and read through some of the job listings. Do any of the jobs *sound* interesting to you? Choose five jobs from each of the areas listed in section 1.2 that interest you and list the responsibilities and qualifications.

Chapter 2

The Measurement and Structure of the National Economy

> Measure what is measurable, and
> make measurable what is not so.
>
> Galileo Galilei

For *millenia*, physicists have sought the *theory of everything*, a hypothetical equation so *robust* that it can explain all physical aspects of the known universe, yet so *elegant*, it would fit on a t-shirt.[1] Macroeconomists have long *had* an equation that captures all *economic* activity and fits on the front of a t-shirt[2]—a theory from which every economic aspect of day-to-day life can be explained and accounted for.

In this chapter, we examine this *economic* theory of everything that is known as *gross domestic product*.

---

[1] For more on the TOE, I recommend Dan Falk *Universe on a T-Shirt* New York: Arcade Books, (2013); and Stephen Hawking *The Universe in a Nutshell* New York: Random House (2001).

[2] I actually had one printed, when I was in grad school, and first taught a macroeconomics class.

2.1   A Brief Historical Note

■ Mercantilists

As we approach the third decade of the twenty-first century, it is long past time we address the way that we measure economic *success*. The *mercantilists* of the sixteenth – eighteenth centuries measured the success/health/power of a nation based on accumulated wealth, as measured by possession of precious metals.[3] The goal, therefore, of all economic activity, of the time, was to accumulate as much wealth as possible.

Nations, under mercantilism, could accumulate wealth in *only* three ways:

1. Mining precious metals
2. Exporting goods & services
3. Stealing precious metals from other countries

Under mercantilism, nations were encouraged to have larger populations. The larger a population, the larger the labor force. The larger the labor force, the more labor available for *mining*[4] and the more goods that could be produced for export in exchange for precious metals.

In the absence of naturally occurring precious metals, imperialism/exploration/piracy were often used to acquire them (e.g., if a European country had no precious metals, they sent explorers to the *New World* to acquire them. If that proved too difficult/costly, they sent ships to rob the *other* European *expolorer's* ships of *their* precious metals)[5]

■ Post-Mercantilists

We have long since abandoned this measure of *wealth* in exchange for a definition basing the success/health/power/*wealth* of a nation on its *productive capability*. Different people use different terms to reference productive capability. Regardless of whether we speak of Full-Employment Output, Long-Run Aggregate Output, or Potential Output, the focus is placed on what a nation is capable of[6] when it efficiently allocates its resources.

---

[3]Gold and silver

[4]Provided the nation has a store of naturally occurring precious metals

[5]For a more in-depth discussion of the rise and fall of mercantilism, refer to Gianni Vaggi and Peter Groenewegen, *A Concise History of Economic Thought* New York: Palgrave Macmillan (2003).

[6]The basis of Adam Smith's *The Wealth of Nations* London: W. Strahan and T. Cadell (1776).

2.2 Gross Domestic Product

Gross domestic product (GDP) is the generally accepted measure of total economic activity within a country, in a given time period.

There are three methods for measuring GDP:

1. Production approach
2. Income approach
3. Expenditure approach

2.2.1 Production Approach

The production approach involves the sum of all value added at the various stages of production and is measured as the *market value of all final goods and services produced in the country in a given time period.*[7] Let us, for a moment, break that statement down.

■ **Market Value**

Given the diversity of goods produced in a country, the easiest way to *include* everything is to not look at the individual goods, but to measure their *value*.
Example:

	Goods Produced	Market Value
1	30 pomelos	$179.70
2	17 automobiles	$510,000
3	27 cookies	$27.00
Total	74 *things*	$510,206.70 worth of *things*

In this example, we see that counting the *things* produced explains little about production activity. If we instead look at the dollar *value* of the goods produced, we have a way to more easily aggregate economic activity. The fact that 74 *things* were produced does not tell us much about the productive capability of the nation. (Were they large things? Were they quality things? What is a *pomelo*?) Rather than talking about *things* we look at *value*.

■ **Final Goods and Services**

Some goods are produced for a final user, and some goods are produced and used in the production of *other* goods. Intermediate goods are used to **add value** to a product, in production.

---

[7]Month, quarter, year

If the US has the capacity to produce 269 million tires[8] in a year, some of those tires are produced and count as *intermediate goods* included in the production of automobiles, and some of those tires are sold directly to customers as a *final good*, replacement tires. If we were to include the tires produced as both intermediate **and** final goods, we would be counting some of the tires more than once. Since this method is concerned *only* with total value added, we look *only* at the final good.

■ **Within a Country**

Since we are interested in the productive capacity of only the domestic economy, we only look at the goods produced *domestically*, regardless of whether the *means of production* are domestically-owned. If we are interested in the value of final goods and services produced by domestically *owned* agents, regardless of whether they are located *in the country*, we would examine the **gross national product**.

2.2.2   Expenditure Approach

The expenditure approach measures economic activity, within the country, by aggregating all spending, or expenditure, in a country, for a given time period. Let us look at the component parts of this aggregate expenditure model.

■ **Consumption Spending** (C_t)

Consumption, which is typically the largest component of GDP, consists of *house-hold* spending on final goods and services. Consumers spend on the following:

1. Durable goods
   Tangible goods that are built to last for many years (e.g., automobiles, furniture, kitchen appliances)

2. Non-durable goods
   Tangible goods made for more immediate use (e.g., clothing, food, toilet tissue)

3. Services
   Intangible transactions, in which the consumer is paying for someone to *do* something *for* the consumer (e.g., accountant, plumber, travel agent)

---

[8]"2018 Facts Section: Plant Capacities," *Modern Tire Dealer*, https://mtd.epubxp.com/i/929435-jan-2018/47?

■ Investment Spending (I_t)

Investment includes any spending, by firms or households, meant to increase capital value. There are three types of investment:

1. Business fixed investment
   Spending by firms on capital (e.g., factory, machinery, tools)

2. Residential fixed investment
   Spending on residential structures (e.g., purchase of a new home, or improvement on a building that is owned by a landlord and rented to tenants)

3. Inventory investment
   Change in the stock of raw materials and finished goods during the year (e.g., an automotive manufacturer may have produced goods during the year that have not sold yet)

■ Government Spending (G_t)

Government spending on final goods and services includes salaries of government workers, military spending, and spending on health care. It is important to recognize that government spending does not include transfer payments, such as Social Security or unemployment benefits, only spending on *actual* goods and services.

■ Net Exports (NX_t)

Net exports, often referred to as the *trade balance*, refer to the difference between goods produced domestically for foreign consumption (exports) and goods produced abroad for domestic consumption (imports.) If a nation's exports exceed imports, we say the nation has a trade *surplus*, and NX adds value to the economy. If a nation's imports exceed exports, we say the nation has a trade *deficit*, and NX subtracts value from the economy.

If a nation is open to international trade, we say that it is an *open* economy, and we include NX in the calculation of GDP; if not, we say that the economy is *closed* and omit NX. A common measure of the level of *openness* of a nation is the quotient[9] of the sum[10] of a nation's exports and imports & GDP.[11]

---

[9]What happens when you divide one thing by another

[10]What happens when you add two things together

[11]$Openness = \frac{Exports_t + Imports_t}{GDP_t}$

■ Putting It Together

Table 2.1: 2018 US GDP (billions of dollars)

Consumption Expenditure	$14,188.40
Investment Expenditure	3,766.30
Government Expenditure	3,569.40
Net Exports	-658.90
Gross Domestic Product	$20,865.10

According to the Bureau of Economic Analysis,[12] US GDP was $20.9 trillion in 2018.

2.2.3   Income Approach

The income approach is calculated by aggregating the factor incomes of the nation's factors of production.

■ **Compensation of employees**
Total wages paid by firms to workers in exchange for their labor

■ **Taxes, less subsidies**
Total government revenue from taxes on production and imports minus subsidies paid

■ **Net operating surplus**
The firm's income after subtracting corporate taxes and expenses.

■ **Consumption of fixed capital**
Defined as the value of the compensation for loss of value of capital assets, due to use, in production.

■ **Statistical discrepancy**
All *income* is derived from *production* therefore, the gross domestic income of a country should equal its gross domestic product. If it does not, that is statistical discrepancy.

---

[12]GDP and the National Income and Product Account (NIPA) Historical Tables, Bureau of Economic Analysis, https://www.bea.gov/data/gdp/gross-domestic-product

■ Putting It Together

Table 2.2: 2018 US GDI (billions of dollars)

Compensation of employees	$10,978.1
Taxes, less subsidies	1,383.7
Net operating surplus	5,137.0
Consumption of fixed capital	3,340.6
Statistical discrepancy	-25.7
Gross domestic income	$20,865.10

Since what we are measuring is total economic activity in a country in a given time period, it should not matter if we are measuring the money *spent*, the amount of income *earned*, or the *value added* at each step of production. As seen in figure 2.1, all three of these measures *must* be equivalent, since the money *spent* by one economic agent is income *earned* by another agent for a good/service that was *produced*. For this reason, GDP is often referred to as *national income* (Y_t).

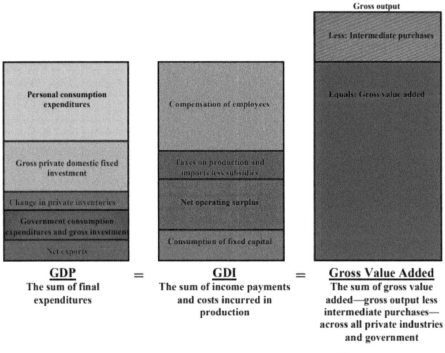

Figure 2.1: Three ways to measure GDP[13]

---

[13]"NIPA Handbook: Concepts and Methods of the US National Income and Product Accounts" Bureau of Economic Analysis, https://www.bea.gov/resources/methodologies/nipa-handbook

2.3   Nominal versus Real

Since we are concerned with the *level* of production, in the nation, we must be careful that the changes we are measuring are due to changes in *output*, not changes in *prices*. For this reason, we distinguish between *nominal* GDP (output valued at *current price levels*) and *real* GDP (output adjusted for differences in price levels.)

$$Nominal\ GDP_t\ =\ Real\ GDP_t \times P_t$$

Figure 2.2 and table 2.3 show US GDP (both nominal and real) since 2000. According to the data, differences in prices account for significant differences between nominal and real GDP.

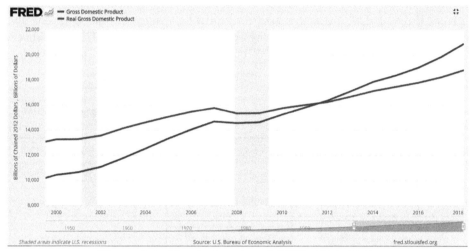

Figure 2.2: Nominal and real GDP, 2000–2018

2.3.1   Real GDP

Since nominal GDP is real GDP **not adjusted for inflation,** we arrive at real GDP by *deflating* nominal GDP.

GDP Deflator

The *GDP deflator* is a means of converting output measured in current prices to GDP with regard to a specific *base year*'s prices. The BEA chose 2012 as the base year. As seen in table 2.3, for 2012 the GDP deflator is approximately 100. Since the GDP deflator for 2018 is approximately 111, we know that 2018 prices are 11 percent higher than 2012 prices.

$$GDP\ Deflator_t = \frac{Nominal\ GDP_t}{Real\ GDP_t} \times 100$$

Table 2.3: US GDP, (billions of dollars)[14]

Year	Nominal GDP	Real GDP	GDP Deflator
2000	$10,439	$13,261	78.72
2001	10,660	13,281	80.27
2002	11,071	13,559	81.65
2003	11,769	14,146	83.20
2004	12,522	14,610	85.71
2005	13,332	15,067	88.49
2006	14,037	15,457	90.82
2007	14,682	15,762	93.15
2008	14,560	15,328	94.99
2009	14,628	15,356	95.26
2010	15,241	15,751	96.76
2011	15,796	16,004	98.70
2012	16,359	16,239	100.74
2013	17,083	16,664	102.52
2014	17,838	17,114	104.23
2015	18,354	17,456	105.15
2016	18,979	17,784	106.72
2017	19,832	18,224	108.82
2018	20,865	18,765	111.19

2.4   Problems with GDP

Despite the fact that GDP *is* the most commonly used measure of economic activity within a country, I would be remiss if I did not point-out that, it does have flaws. Let us look at a few of them:

- Non-Market Transactions
  Non-market transactions, which are not provided for pay, (e.g., household work,) do not count toward GDP. Even if production takes place, if it is not for pay, it is not counted.

When I was an undergraduate, my introductory macroeconomics Professor told a story that went something like this:

I, being a young unmarried professor, purchase a new home and hire three people: a housekeeper, a chef, and a gardener. One day, I am sick and decide to stay home and sleep, forgetting that it is the housekeeper's day to come in and clean. Upon finding me at home (and unwell) she makes me some soup, we fall madly

---

[14]Gross Domestic Product https://www.bea.gov/data/gdp/gross-domestic-product

in love, she quits her job, and we marry in the spring.

After we are married, she informs me that, being a better cook, she would like to do all the cooking, so we fire the cook.

When we return from our honeymoon, she informs me that it has always been her dream to have a garden of her own, so we fire the gardener.

The cleaning, the cooking, and the gardening are STILL being done; however, since no one is getting paid, none of it counts toward the measure of GDP.

■ The Sustainability Problem

The growth in production that a nation exhibits *could* be due to a depletion of resources in the country, meaning that the high GDP is non-sustainable.

Let us say that a mainly agrarian nation discovers oil. Suddenly, their GDP increases dramatically, due to oil being valued more highly than agriculture. What is *not* reflected by GDP is that the oil is a *finite* resource that runs out in five years.

■ The Environmental Problem

What if the finite *resource* is the environment? Depleting natural resources today, leaves nothing for the future. This may benefit a nation's macroeconomic image; on paper, however, that will be short-lived.

■ International Data Comparison Problem

International macroeconomic data comparison is a lot like sports talk radio, in any major city. Someone calls in to a drive-time program and states that "the New York Yankees are the best team in Major League Baseball."

Someone *else* calls in and argues that "the Boston Red Sox are the best team in Major League Baseball."

The "conversation" soon devolves into a screaming match of statistics. "Look at the batting." "Consider the pitching!" "More titles than any team in history!" "More titles in the twenty-first century!" "CURSED!!!"

Depending on the statistics examined, they both claim victory. With international data comparison, it is the same. You will often hear people speak of which nation has the "strongest" economy. If we use GDP, we get one answer, to which people may respond, "What about standard of living?" And at this point someone else may reply, "What about the environment?"

According to some economists,[15] international macroeconomic data comparison is
impossible due to how nations *handle* their data.[16]

2.5 Alternative Price Indices

Given the multidimensional nature of a nation's economy, there are multiple measures of inflation. Why should consumers be concerned with changes in the price
of goods that only affect producers or the government? When there are increases
in the price of the McDonnell Douglas F-15 Eagle, consumers do not directly experience this price increase, since a fighter jet is not a consumer good.

Since the GDP deflator concerns itself with how inflation affects the *entire* economy,[17] we look to measures that directly address inflation's impact on consumers.[18]

2.5.1 Consumer Price Index

The Consumer Price Index is a measure of how consumers experience inflation.
To calculate CPI, we take a fixed basket of consumer goods and measure how
its price changes over time. The basket is weighted, as seen in Figure 2.3, with
Housing and *Transportation* being the largest two components, making-up more
than half of consumer goods.

$$Consumer\ Price\ Index_t = \frac{Market\ Basket_t}{Market\ Basket_{base\ year}} \times 100$$

[15]Morgenstern, Oskar. *On the Accuracy of Economic Observations*. Princeton, NJ: Princeton University Press, 1963.
Reagle, Derrick, and Dominick Salvatore. "Robustness of Forecasting Financial Crises in Emerging Market Economies with Data Revisions – A Note." *Open Economies Review* 16, no. 2 (2005): 209–16.
Santangelo, Giacomo. "International Data Revision: Theory and Analysis." *Asian Journal of Public Affairs* 1, no. 1 (2007): 7–19.
[16]In constructing the US GDP tables, for this chapter, I was forced to make *significant* changes, due to the US BEA *updating* the 2018 data. If you compare the data I have recorded and compare it to the current BEA data for 2018, it may be different.
[17]Consumers, firms, and government
[18]Us

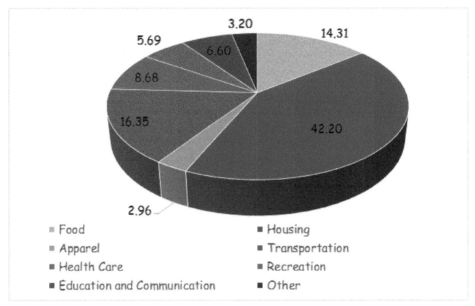

Figure 2.3: Consumer Price Index

Some analysts criticize the calculation of CPI based on its use of fixed weights. Fixed weights, they believe, prevent the CPI from accurately reflecting:

- the introduction of new goods,
- the substitution of higher-quality goods,
- the substitution of cheaper goods,
- changes in how consumers shop (discount outlets, wholesale clubs).

These omissions lead to the overstatement of CPI by about 1 percent per year.

2.5.2   Personal Consumption Expenditures Price Index

The Personal Consumption Expenditure Price Index (PCEPI) is an alternate measure of how consumers experience inflation. It measures the prices paid for all goods and services that consumers *actually* purchase.

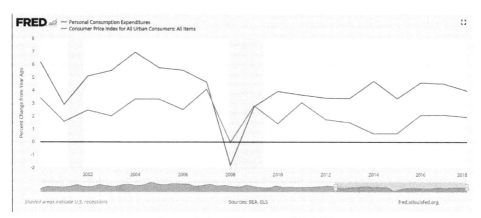

Figure 2.4: CPI versus PCEPI

Unlike the CPI, which fixes a basket of goods with predetermined weights that
do not change over time for several years, the PCEPI includes *all* goods in the
amounts that people consume them. In figure 2.4 we see that the CPI tends
to be more stable. In the absence of the fixed weights, the PCEPI shows more
sensitivity to changes in consumer prices.

2.6   Popular Macroeconomic Data Sources

■ https://www.bea.gov/
■ https://www.bls.gov/
■ https://www.cia.gov/library/publications/resources/the-world-factbook/
■ https://fred.stlouisfed.org/
■ https://www.imf.org/en/Data
■ https://data.worldbank.org/

Food for Thought

1. How does our current definition of wealth differ from that of the mercantilists? How is it similar?

2. Why does it not matter which approach is used to measure economic activity?

3. Go to your favorite macroeconomic data source,[19] choose any three countries
   and calculate their *openness* index.

4. Go to the Bureau of Economic Analysis website. What is the current US
   real GDP? How does it differ from nominal GDP? What does this suggest?

---

[19] Doesn't everyone have one of those? No? Just me?

5. Why do some economists believe international macroeconomic data comparison so difficult?

6. What issues are raised by the use of *fixed weights* in measuring CPI?

7. Why do some analysts prefer PCEPI to CPI?

Chapter 3

National Income Accounting: Productivity, Output, and Employment

Now that we know *how* we are measuring economic activity, let's take a closer look at *what* we are measuring.

$$Y_t = C_t + I_t + G_t + NX_t$$

In measuring national income (Y_t) using the aggregate expenditure approach, we can divide the formula into the level of output of goods and services (on the left) and the *demand* for that output, as measured by spending (on the right.) This chapter will focus on the *left* side of the equation, what many call national income, which we will, for now, call *total output*.

To understand *total output*, we must discuss the process by which all things are made, beginning with *inputs*.

■ Productive Resources

When we discuss productive resources in economics, classically we are speaking about three things:

1. Land
2. Labor
3. Capital

Anything that can be considered a *gift of nature*, (e.g., arable land, minerals, things provided by the earth) is counted as *land* (e.g., the 72,000 acres of NJ farmland used in 2018[1] for the production of corn, is counted as land).

Labor refers to the *human effort* utilized to transform the other resources into a finished product (e.g., the labor force of the United States, in January 2018 was approximately 163 million people[2]).

Capital[3] is defined as a resource whose accumulation, through investment, increases productive capacity. There are three types of capital, in which we invest:

1. Physical capital
2. Financial capital
3. Human capital

Physical capital consists of machinery, buildings, and equipment used in production (e.g., a combine harvester used by a farmer, or the collaborative robotics used by an automotive manufacturer).

Financial capital consists of internal retained earnings or money borrowed or invested, used to assist in the increase of the capital value of the firm (e.g., the money raised from the issuing of bonds, stock, or directly borrowed from a bank).

Human capital[4] is the education, training, experience, and skill-set of the labor force.

In economics, we distinguish between the *short* and *long* run. The *long run* is a time period so long that all productive inputs are variable, and all prices are flexible. The *short run* concentrates on the behavior of variables over the time period of a few years, during which it is believed that some inputs, like capital, are fixed, wages are *rigid*, and prices are *sticky*.

---

[1] US Department of Agriculture, https://www.nass.usda.gov/

[2] US Bureau of Labor Statistics, http://www.bls.gov

[3] For an exhaustive discussion of capital, see Thomas Piketty *Capital in the Twenty-First Century* (Cambridge, MA: Belknap Press, 2017).

[4] See Gary S. Becker, *Human Capital: A Theoretical and Empirical Analysis with Special Reference to Education* (Cambridge, MA: National Bureau of Economic Research, 1994).

3.1 Production Function

A production function is the functional relationship that explains how changes in the quantity of productive resources affect the quantity of output.[5] In this way, we can say that output is a function of the level of technology, or total factor productivity, and the value of capital and the number of labor-hours used in production at a given period in time.

$$Y_t = F(A_t, K_t, L_t)$$

■ Putting It Together

As we saw in chapter 2, in 2018, the level of technology (A_t), the stock of capital (K_{2018}), and the stock of labor (L_{2018}) available in the US produced $Y_{2018} = $20,865$ billion worth of output.

3.1.1 The Cobb–Douglas Production Function

For the purposes of this discussion, we look at a *specific* production function called the Cobb–Douglas production function, which allows us to examine the responsiveness of output to changes in the levels of capital and labor. (e.g., a 1 percent increase in labor would increase output by β percent)

$$Y_t = F(A, K_t, L_t) = A_t K_t^{\alpha} L_t^{\beta}$$

3.1.2 Returns to Scale

In microeconomics, when we discuss Production Theory, we refer to *returns to scale* with regard to the relationship between a firm's long-run costs and the level of output in the *Three Stages of Production:*

1. Increasing returns to scale
2. Constant returns to scale
3. Decreasing returns to scale

Figure 3.1 illustrates an example of long-run production cost. *Increasing returns to scale* occur when the per-unit cost (long-run average total cost) decreases, as the level of output increases. This is seen as the production from 1,000 to 5,000 units. *Constant returns to scale* occur when the per-unit cost remains the same, as the level of output increases. The region of production exhibiting constant returns is the period for which the productive process is the most efficient, as the firm is able to *increase* its level of production without incurring any additional costs. Output from 5,000 to 6,000 units exhibits constant returns. *Decreasing returns to*

---

[5]What *microeconomists* refer to as *total product*

scale occur when the per-unit cost increases as the scale of production is increased. Production of more than 6,000 units can be seen to exhibit decreasing returns.

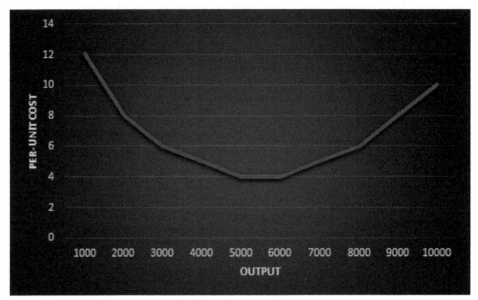

Figure 3.1: Long-run average cost curve

In macroeconomics, we discuss *returns to scale* to express how much additional output will be produced when all factors of production are increased proportionally. Returning to the Cobb–Douglas function we can express this by examining α & β:

$$Y_t = A_t K_t^\alpha L_t^\beta$$

When $\alpha + \beta > 1$, the production function displays *increasing* returns to scale, meaning that increasing capital and labor by 1 percent will increase output by *more than* 1 percent. When $\alpha + \beta < 1$, returns to scale are *decreasing*, and when $\alpha + \beta = 1$, the production exhibits *constant* returns to scale. For the purposes of our analysis, we assume a Cobb–Douglas production function with constant returns to scale. An example of this can be written as

$$Y_t = A_t K_t^{0.5} L_t^{0.5}$$

In the *long run* this is graphically represented by figure 3.2.

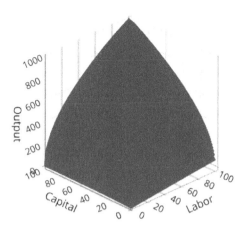

Figure 3.2: Cobb–Douglas production function with variable inputs

Figure 3.2 illustrates changes in the level of output when both capital and labor
are variable. To understand the dynamics of the production process, let us look at
the effect of changes in output, when we vary labor inputs, holding capital inputs
constant.

$$Y_t = \bar{A}_t \bar{K}_t^{0.5} L_t^{0.5}$$

3.2   The Demand for Labor

Demand is defined as the relationship between the price of a good or service and
the quantity that someone plans to buy. Generally, this relationship is negative,
as the price of a good *increases* the quantity demanded *decreases*. The decision
to demand a good or service at a specific price is based on the perceived benefit
that will be gained from the use of the good or service.[6]

On a microeconomic level, we discuss *individual* demand and *market* demand,
recognizing that *market* demand the aggregation of all individual demand.

When discussing the labor market, it is important to note that the *good* in question is labor and it is being *demanded* by the firms that will employ it to produce
goods and services.

---

[6]Is this good or service *worth it?*

3.2.1   The Economic Problem of the Typical Firm

In order to discuss the aggregate labor market, we must, for the time being, discuss the behavior of the *typical firm*. The economy is comprised of *very* many typical firms, each having the same goal, **profit maximization**.

$$\max_{L}\{PY - WL\}$$

Given the number of firms in the economy, the typical firm has influence over neither the *price* it receives for the goods/services it produces, nor the *wage* it must pay labor. The firm will continue to hire labor to maximize profit. In deciding the number of laborers that a firm will hire, it must examine the total *benefit* it will receive from the hiring of additional labor. The *benefit* to the firm is measured by labor's contribution to total product. The firm will continue to hire workers, until the benefit received is equal to the *cost* of labor. Figure 3.3 illustrates how output increases as labor increases, holding capital and technology constant.

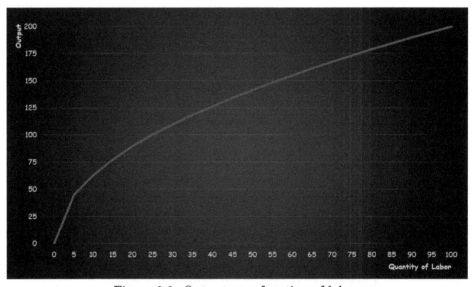

Figure 3.3: Output as a function of labor

3.2.2   Marginal Product of Labor and Labor Demand

From an economic perspective, all decisions are made *at the margin*. The *marginal product of labor* is defined as the *additional* benefit that firms receive from the hiring of an *additional* unit of labor and can be expressed as the change in Y as L increases.

$$MP_L = \tfrac{\Delta Y}{\Delta L} = F(\bar{K}_t, L_t + 1) - F(\bar{K}t, L_t)$$

With regard to the general form of the Cobb–Douglas production function, we can
calculate the marginal product of labor by taking the partial derivative of output
with respect to labor:

$$MP_L = \beta A_t K_t^\alpha L_t^{\beta-1}$$

This can be re-written as:

$$MP_L = \beta\left(\frac{A_t K_t^\alpha L_t^\beta}{L}\right)$$

which simplifies to β multiplied by the average product of labor:

$$MP_L = \beta\left(\frac{Y_t}{L_t}\right)$$

While figure 3.3 illustrates that as labor increases, output increases, figure 3.4
shows that as more labor input is added, output increases *at a decreasing rate*.
In other words, each additional worker contributes less to the productive process
than the worker hired before. This is known as the *law of diminishing marginal
returns*. It is defined as the decrease in the rate at which output *increases* as the
amount of a single productive factor input of production is increased. Marginal
product of labor diminishes because by holding all *other* factors constant, as labor
increases, each worker has less access to the fixed amount of capital. Therefore,
the *value* of each additional worker *decreases* as more workers are added.

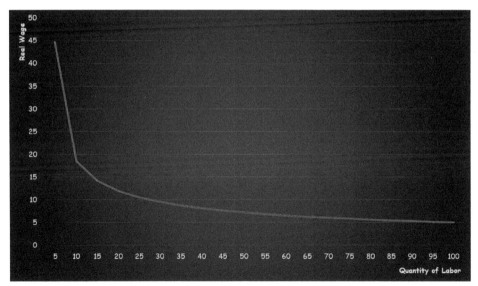

Figure 3.4: Marginal product of labor

Since the marginal product of labor is the measure of the additional output given
an additional worker, in order to calculate the *nominal* or money *Wage*, we take
the marginal product of labor and multiply it by the price of the good/service.

$$W = MP_L \times P$$

The nominal wage relates how the revenue of the firm is affected by the contribution of the additional worker.

The labor demand, being a demand function, expresses the inverse relationship between quantity of labor that firms are willing to hire and the cost of labor, the *real wage rate*.

Since prices are determined in the market and subject to change, the firm's decision to hire labor is not based on the nominal wage. In order to understand the firm's demand for labor, we must look to the *real wage* ($\frac{W}{P}$) which is expressed, not in money terms, but is measured in units of output. The real wage is the nominal wage adjusted for inflation and is an expression of the *marginal cost* of labor to producers. As the real wage increases, labor becomes more expensive and the quantity demanded decreases, causing a movement *along* the demand curve. For this reason, the demand curve for labor is identical to the MP_L curve in figure 3.4, and labor will continue to be hired until the marginal product of labor is equal to the real wage. Since changes in the number of workers account for movements along the production function, which, in turn, cause movements *along* the labor demand curve, we must look elsewhere for factors that cause a *shift* in production and labor demand.

3.2.3   Factors Shifting the Demand Curve for Labor

There are two factors responsible for shifting labor demand:

- Changes in productivity (A)
- Changes in the stock of capital (K)

If there is an increase in either the productivity of labor or an increase in the capital accumulated, two outcomes are seen: (1) The same number of laborers produce a larger quantity of output, and (2) the real wage increases, due to each laborer being, now, worth more to the firm. Both of these increases can be seen in figure 3.5 as the production function shifts up and the labor demand shifts out.

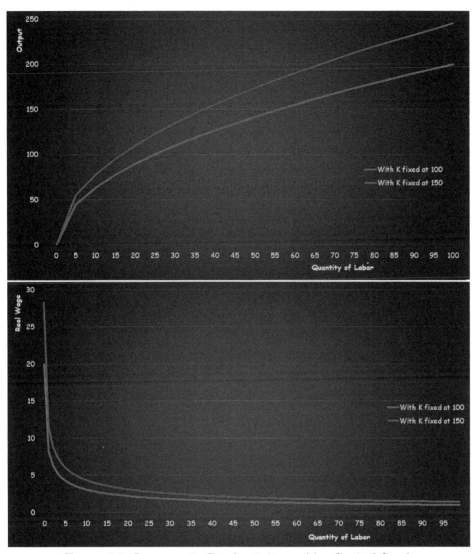

Figure 3.5: Increases in Productivity and/or Capital Stock

3.3 The Supply of Labor

Supply is defined as the relationship between the price of a good or service and
the quantity that a supply is willing to produce. Generally, this is a positive relationship, as the price increases, suppliers are willing to produce a larger quantity.

3.3.1   Long Run versus Short Run

In the long-run, it is believed that the supply of labor is *perfectly price inelastic*; in other words, the quantity of labor supplied is *not* affected by the level of wages. The long-run labor supply curve is represented by a vertical line. We also believe that the long-run level of labor will be fixed at, what is known as *full employment.*[7] The short-run supply of labor is a different story. In the short run, workers have to make a labor supply decision, choosing how many hours of labor they are willing to supply in the market.

3.3.2   The Economic Problem of the Typical Laborer

There were approximately 163 million people in the US labor force in December 2018.[8] Each individual one of these laborers was faced with the same decision. If we examine one of these *typical* workers, we can see how the labor supply decision functions.

It is a truth universally acknowledged that people seek to maximize the level of satisfaction that they receive in life. In economics, this satisfaction is referred to as *utility.* People gain utility through consumption activities. Due to the cost of some of these activities, individuals seek income. Workers earn income from their labor. The more labor hours they provide, the more income labor earns. The more income the laborer earns, the more consumption activity the laborer can take part in; however, the typical laborer also receives utility from *not* working. This is known as the *labor-leisure trade-off.*

$$\max_{N} U = F(wN,\ L)$$

where N is the number of labor hours, L is the number of leisure hours, and w is the wage. The typical laborer will choose the quantity of L that maximizes his or her utility.

In order for a laborer to decide to offer his or her labor in the market, the benefit that he or she perceives that he or she will receive from working must outweigh the perceived benefit from *not* working. The laborer must, therefore, choose the combination of work and leisure that will maximize his or her utility. Typically, the only way that a laborer will give-up an hour of leisure is if the wage increases. Economist Gary Becker observes that "the allocation and efficiency of non-working may . . . be more important to economic welfare than that of working time."[9]

---

[7]We will discuss this concept further, in a later section.

[8]Bureau of Labor Statistics, https://www.bls.gov/

[9]Becker, Gary S., "A Theory of the Allocation of Time." *The Economic Journal* 75, no. 299 (1965): 493–517, 493

3.3.3   The Real Wage and the Supply of Labor

Since the short-run supply of labor is elastic, the higher the real wage, the more labor hours people are willing to supply. This is true despite the two opposing forces at work.

When the real wage increases, if workers wish to increase income, they substitute an hour of working, for an hour of leisure. For this reason, when the real wage increases, people offer up more labor, and the quantity of labor supplied increases. This is known as the *substitution effect*. However, when the real wage increases, the worker has an incentive to work the *same* number of hours, or if the worker wishes to maintain his or her *current* income, the worker may work *fewer* hours, leading to a *decrease* in the supply of labor. This is called the *income effect*. Given that one effect causes a movement *along* the line, and the other a *shift,* it is important to pay attention to what the increase in the real wage may represent to the worker.

3.3.4   Factors Shifting the Supply Curve for Labor

We have already seen the effect of an increase in the real wage when the income effect outweighs the substitution effect, but why does that happen? Part of the reason stems from the fact that the labor-leisure question is one of intertemporal substitution. In making the decision to work in the current time period, the worker must consider, not only his or her *current* leisure, but also how much leisure he or she can have in the *future* if the real wage remains *high*. Because the worker expects *future* wages to be higher, he or she needs to supply *fewer* hours to the market, shifting the supply of labor in.

The other reason for the income effect overpowering the substitution effect is the rising real wage's effect on *wealth*. Literally, the higher the real wage, the more the worker's ability to accumulate wealth. The greater the amount of wealth, the fewer hours of labor the worker need supply, causing the curve to shift in.

3.4   Labor Market Equilibrium

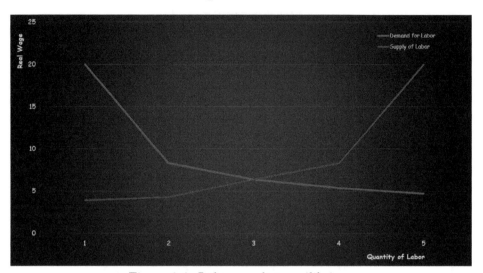

Figure 3.6: Labor market equilibrium

In equilibrium, the quantity of labor demanded by firms equals the quantity of labor that workers are willing to supply. This determines the equilibrium values of the real wage and employment. When the market is in equilibrium, barring outside forces, the market will remain in equilibrium.

If the real wage is too high, we find a surplus of labor, which will force the real wage *down*, increasing the quantity demand for labor and decreasing the quantity of supply, bringing the market back into equilibrium. Likewise, with a real wage that is below equilibrium, the shortage of labor will force the real wage *up*, increasing laborers' willingness to work, bringing the market back into equilibrium.

3.4.1   Wages in the Short Run

As mentioned earlier, in the short run, wages are believed *rigid*, meaning they do *not* adjust in order to equilibrate supply and demand, causing a surplus of labor. Historically, there are three reasons for rigid wages:

1. Unions and collective bargaining agreements
   As Lindbeck and Snower explain in their 1989 book,[10] workers represented by labor unions (insiders) exercise their market power to keep wages high. These higher than market clearing wages adversely affect the unemployed

---

[10]Assar Lindbeck and Dennis Snower, *The Insider-Outsider Theory of Employment and Unemployment* (Cambridge, MA: MIT Press, 1989).

and non-union workers (outsiders) who would *settle* for the, relatively lower, equilibrium wage.

2. Efficiency wages
   As discusssed by Krueger and Summers,[11] higher wages may be effective at increasing worker productivity by eliciting better performance through reduced turnover and increased effort.

3. Minimum wage laws
   Basic supply and demand theory suggests that price controls are one of the contributing factors to *market failure*.[12] Since a minimum wage is a *price floor*,[13] increases in the minimum wage are expected to decrease the demand for labor, increasing unemployment.[14]

■ Putting It Together

As previously stated, we believe that the market is comprised of very many typical firms and typical laborers, so when we aggregate the individual behavior of these firms and laborers, we end-up with the **aggregate labor market**, which is used to determine the level of production, in the economy.

3.4.2   Full-Employment GDP

Since the quantity of output is determined by the level of technology, the quantity of capital stock (which we are holding constant, for the time being) and labor, the level of output at which the labor market is *in equilibrium* (Y^*), is dependent on the *full-employment* level of the labor force L^*. To this end, it is the goal of most policy to reach the full-employment level of output.[15]

$$Y_t^* = F(\bar{A}_t, \bar{K}_t, L_t^*)$$

Given that the full-employment level of output is dependent on equilibrium in the aggregate labor market, anything that shifts the production function[16] or labor's willingness to work will affect the full-employment or potential level of output in the economy. However, when the economy is *at* full employment it does not mean that rate of unemployment in the economy is equal to zero, an issue we will examine in the next section.

---

[11] Alan B. Krueger and Lawrence H. Summers, "Efficiency Wages and the Inter-Industry Wage Structure," *Econometrica* 56, no. 2 (1988): 259–293.

[12] The situation in which a free market leads to an inefficient allocation of resources (e.g., unemployment).

[13] A minimum price, below which, the market price cannot be allowed to fall.

[14] David Card and Alan B. Krueger, *Myth and Measurement: The New Economics of the Minimum Wage* (Princeton, NJ : Princeton University Press, 1995)

[15] also referred to as full-employment GDP, long-run GDP, or long-run aggregate supply.

[16] Technological change, change in the stock of capital

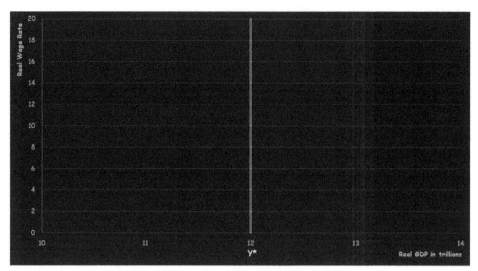

Figure 3.7: Full-Employment GDP

As we see in figure 3.7, at the equilibrium level of labor, in our example, full-employment GDP is roughly $11 trillion and is perfectly price inelastic (i.e., regardless of changes in prices, when the resources are fully-employed, the nation produces at its potential).

3.5   Unemployment

Given the influence that labor has on output, joblessness clearly is a concern. If the economy is not operating at full-employment, it is not producing its optimal level of output.

The Bureau of Labor Statistics (BLS) is the government agency in the US Department of Labor responsible for measuring and monitoring US unemployment. According to the BLS, people are *unemployed*

> if they do not have a job, have actively looked for work in the prior 4 weeks, and are currently available for work. Persons who were not working and were waiting to be recalled to a job from which they had been temporarily laid off are also included as unemployed.[17]

---

[17]Bureau of Labor Statistics, "Labor Force Characteristics from the Current Population Survey," https://www.bls.gov/cps/lfcharacteristics.htm#unemp

3.5.1   Measuring Unemployment

Every month, the US Bureau of the Census conducts the *Current Population Survey* of US households and records labor force characteristics for the BLS. Among these data, the survey records the size of the labor force, the number of employed, the number of people who are unemployed, and the number of people *not in the labor force.*

To be considered *not in the labor force* and therefore not included in the calculation of labor market activity, a person must be neither employed nor seeking employment. These people may be retired, be students, or be hospitalized or not working for some other reason. Because of the existence of people *not in the labor force*, the reported official unemployment percentage (referred to as U-3) can be *misleading.* If a person looks for work for an extended period of time and is unable to find work, the BLS considers him or her a *marginally attached worker* and stops counting him or her in the labor force. The marginally attached fall into two categories, those who have stopped looking and those who are still seeking employment.

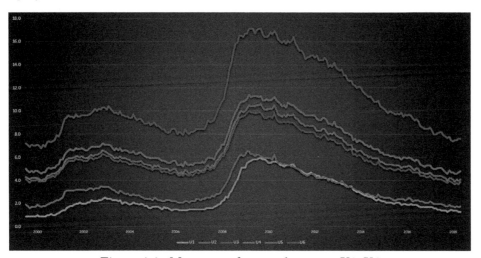

Figure 3.8: Measures of unemployment, U1–U6

As can be seen in figure 3.8, depending on the measure that is used, estimates of unemployment vary a great deal. As previously stated, U-3, the *official unemployment rate*, which is reported in the media regularly, counts all unemployed persons in the labor force; however, U-6 includes not only the unemployed, but also the marginally attached and people who are working part time only because they cannot find full-time work. The figure shows that all six measures are correlated, meaning that they all move together.

In addition to U1–U6, the BLS also reports on the size of the labor force relative to the working-age population. *Labor force participation*, seen in figure 3.9, is the quotient[18] of the labor force and the number of non-institutionalized people who are of working-age. Taken together, it can be observed that while unemployment has fluctuated in the first two decades of the twenty-first century, labor force participation has steady declined.

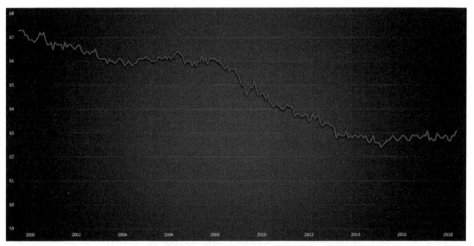

Figure 3.9: Labor force participation

There is clearly more to unemployment than many people may expect. When presented with changes in unemployment, one would be wise to see what those changes are reflecting. For more on the various *alternative* measures of unemployment, I recommend investigating the BLS website.

3.5.2 Types of Unemployment

Economists recognize three types of unemployment:

1. Frictional unemployment
   Frictional unemployment occurs when a person is *between* jobs. Since most people are not looking for work until they become unemployed, it will naturally take time to find a new job. It is believed that the frictionally unemployed will find a new job; it is only a matter of looking.

2. Structural unemployment
   A person becomes structurally unemployed when the job that he or she has is no longer valued due to a decrease in the demand for the good/service he or she was producing or a change in technology such that fewer workers are

---

[18]That's what happens when you divide one thing by another.

required to do the job. The structurally unemployed tend to have a harder time finding work. If the job loss is due to technological progress, it may require the worker to return to school for training in a field that the labor market values.

3. Cyclical unemployment
   Cyclical unemployment exists because of the normal working of the economy. When there is a slowdown in spending, fewer workers are required to produce goods, therefore unemployment increases. When the economy recovers, it is expected that unemployment will fall.

In the absence of cyclical unemployment, joblessness is due to frictional and structural unemployment, which are normal in a dynamic economy. If this is the case, unemployment is said to be at its *natural rate*. Full employment is said to exist when unemployment is at it natural rate. At this level of unemployment, the economy is producing the full-employment level of output.

The natural rate of unemployment, then, can be viewed as the rate of unemployment *around which* the economy can comfortably function. When unemployment is *above* its natural rate, the economy is operating below full employment and not producing its full-potential level of output. When unemployment is *below* its natural rate, the economy is producing *beyond* its potential and we risk inflation. Figure 3.10 shows the relationship between unemployment and its natural rate.

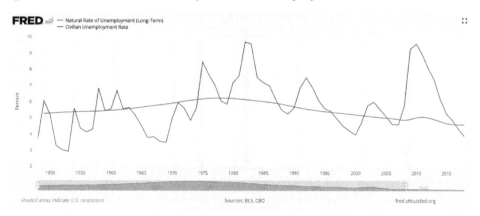

Figure 3.10: Cyclical unemployment

3.6   Relating Output and Employment

The effect that increases in unemployment have on overall output are of particular interest. All too often, people are concerned with unemployment's effect on *current* GDP, however, we must also consider the effect that it has on *future* GDP.

3.6.1   Okun's Law

When unemployment increases, output falls below its potential level. The amount below its potential that GDP falls tends to follow the general rule called *Okun's law*. Named for Arthur Okun, the law relates the changes in full-employment GDP relative to changes in unemployment. According to Okun, the growth rate of real GDP will be equal to the growth rate of potential GDP so long as there is no change in unemployment. For every 1 percent increase in unemployment, real GDP growth falls by ω percent.

$$\frac{\Delta Y}{Y} = \frac{\Delta Y*}{Y*} - \omega \Delta U_t$$

Using data from the Federal Reserve Bank of St. Louis, regression analysis can be used to estimate the parameters of Okun's law. Regressing quarterly data on the percent change in real GDP and the change in unemployment,

$$\frac{\Delta Y}{Y} = \alpha + \beta(\Delta U_t)$$

where α is the growth rate of potential GDP and β is the effect that changes in unemployment are expected to have on GDP.

Historically, α and β have been found to be approximately 3 percent and -2, respectively. This would mean that, in the absence of changes in unemployment, potential GDP grows at an average of 3 percent per year, and for every 1 percent increase in unemployment, the growth rate of real GDP falls by 2 percent.

Using quarterly data for 1949 through 2018, we are able to construct figure 3.11 and run the accompanying regression. Both the figure and the regression support that a negative relationship *does* exist between changes in unemployment and the growth rate of GDP. From the regression, we see that between 1949 and 2018 the estimated growth rate of potential GDP is 3.2 percent and the Okun coefficient is -1.8, supporting Okun's law.

$$\frac{\Delta Y}{Y} = 3.2 - 1.8\Delta U_t$$

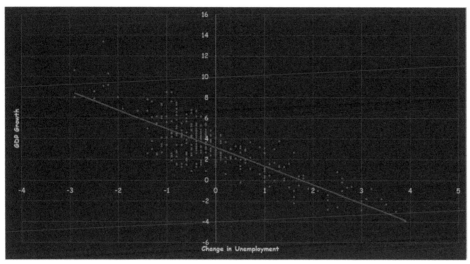

Figure 3.11: Okun's law

3.6.2   The Lucas Wedge

The total loss in GDP for an economy resulting from a slowdown in the growth rate of real GDP, is referred to as the *Lucas wedge*. Named for economist Robert Lucas, the Lucas wedge represents the cost to society because of the inefficiency of the market and is calculated by examining the difference between potential GDP and real GDP. Unlike Okun's law, which focuses on how changes in unemployment affect GDP growth, the Lucas wedge deals with the *accumulation* of loss as a result of the actual growth rate falling below the potential growth rate, asking the question, How much more might the economy have produced, if not for the slowdown?

Food for Thought

1. Using online resources, what is the current size of the US labor force?

2. How many people were unemployed last month?

3. Is unemployment above or below the natural rate?

4. What is the most recent labor force participation rate?

5. Using data from the FRED[19] database, estimate the Okun's Law coefficient for the years since 2000.

---

[19] Federal Reserve Bank of St. Louis, https://fred.stlouisfed.org/

6. What is the expected growth rate of potential GDP? Is it different than that of 1949–2018. What does this mean?

7. Why might an increase in the real wage decrease the number of labor hours the typical laborer chooses to supply?

Chapter 4

National Income Accounting: Consumption, Savings, Investment, and Government Spending

As we covered in chapter 3, we can take the aggregate expenditure model, $Y_t = C_t + I_t + G_t + NX_t$, as a measure of the supply and demand for all goods and services produced in a nation, in a given time period. To this end, since we take the supply to be determined by the production of goods and services, we look to the right side of the equation for the demand, as measured by spending.

For the purposes of the next few chapters, we will consider only spending on and within the *domestic* economy, examining a *closed economy*, in which there is no international sector. To that end, we define GDP for a closed economy as

$$Y_t = C_t + I_t + G_t$$

Therefore, for the time being, total spending in the economy consists *only* of consumption, investment, and government spending.

4.1   Consumption Expenditure

As we learn in microeconomics, consumption spending is assumed dependent on disposable income. We define *disposable income* as total personal income minus taxes $(Y - T)$. At higher levels of disposable income, we expect higher levels of consumption spending. The extent to which disposable income affects consumption, however, depends on the economic theory to which you subscribe. In this section, we examine the most popular consumption theory, the *Keynesian consumption function.*

4.1.1   Keynesian Consumption

In 1936, economist John Maynard Keynes wrote in *The General Theory of Employment, Interest and Money*:

> We . . . define what we shall call *the propensity to consume* as the functional relationship between . . . Y, a given level of income . . . and C the expenditure on consumption out of that level of income, so that $C = f(Y)$.
>
> The amount that the community spends on consumption obviously depends (i) partly on the amount of its income, (ii) partly on other objective attendant circumstances, and (iii) partly on the subjective needs and the psychological propensities and habits of the individuals composing it.
>
> The fundamental psychological law, upon which we are entitled to depend with great confidence both *a priori* from our knowledge of human nature and from the detailed facts of experience, is that men are disposed, as a rule and on average, to increase their consumption as their income increases, but not by as much as the increase in their income. That is . . . $\frac{dC}{dY}$ is positive and less than unity.[1]

In other words . . .

The theory postulates a stable relationship between consumption and income

$$C = C(Y)$$

and claims that the proportion of income that a consumer will spend, the *marginal propensity to consume*, is between 0 and 1.

---

[1] John Maynard Keynes, *The General Theory of Employment, Interest and Money* (London: Palgrave Macmillan, 1936).

$$0 < \beta < 1$$

The Keynesian model of consumption is, therefore

$$C = \alpha + \beta Y + \epsilon$$

where α reflects non-income related determinants of consumption and the marginal propensity to consume (β) measures how consumption (C) responds to changes in income(Y).

Keynes and the Real World

As Keynes states, people make spending (and by default, savings) decisions that drive consumption expenditure. The wages, dividends, interest, and rents that households receive are all counted as *household income*. Once taxes are paid on all the sources of income, what is left is *disposable income*. Consumers spend a portion of their disposable income, their marginal propensity to consume (MPC), on consumption, and *save* the rest, such that the *sum* of the marginal propensities to consume and save is one.

$$MPC + MPS = 1$$

Disposable income changes if either national income (real GDP) or net taxes change. If real GDP increases or net taxes decrease, we expect consumption spending to increase. If real GDP falls or net taxes increase, we expect consumption spending to fall. The extent to which this happens, according to Keynes, is the MPC.

Using monthly US data on real disposable personal income (DSPIC96) and real personal consumption expenditure (PCEC96), for the time period January 2002 through January 2019, we are able to construct figure 4.1 and estimate values for α and β.

$$C(Y_t - T_t) = 859.74 + 0.8332(Y_t - T_t)$$

A marginal propensity to consume of 0.8332 means that for every additional \$1 increase in disposable income, consumption spending increases by an average of \$0.83, while *savings* increases by approximately \$0.17, supporting Keynes's theory that MPC is positive and less than 1.

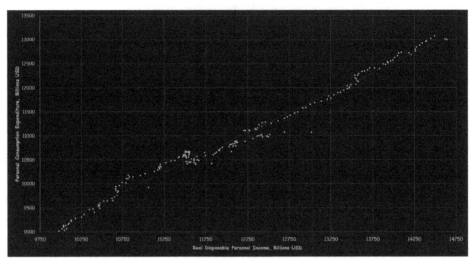

Figure 4.1: Keynesian consumption function

4.2 Investment Expenditure

Investment includes any spending, by firms or households, meant to increase capital value. Investment is a *very* complex topic that is often times *over*simplified when taught at the undergraduate level. Students are told that investment is a function of the real interest rate, $I_t = I(r_t)$, but not told how. While it is *true* that investment is negatively related to the real interest rate, there is more to investment that that. I believe that we can address a more *realistic* approach, explaining *how* and *why* the real interest rate influences the investment decision, without losing focus.

As we discussed in chapter 2, there are three types of investment expenditure, as seen in figure 4.2:

1. Business fixed investment
   Spending by firms on capital (e.g., factory, machinery, tools)

2. Residential fixed investment
   Spending on residential structures (e.g., purchase of a new home or improvement on a building that is owned by a landlord and rented to tenants)

3. Inventory investment
   Change in the stock of raw materials and finished goods during the year (e.g., an automotive manufacturer may have produced goods, during the year that have not sold yet.)

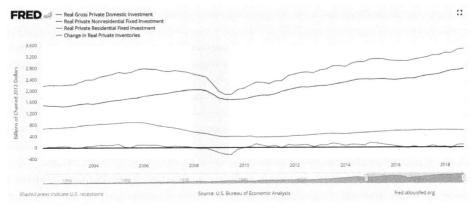

Figure 4.2: US investment expenditure, 2002–2018

4.2.1 Business Fixed Investment

In order to understand the mechanics of the largest portion of investment, business investment, (what the BEA refers to as *real private nonresidential fixed investment*) one must consider that, in an attempt to maximize profit, in very much the same way that firms continue to hire labor until the marginal benefit of the last worker, MP_L, is equal to the cost of labor, $\frac{W}{P}$, firms will make the decision to continue to *rent* capital until the marginal benefit of the last unit of capital, MP_K, is equal to the real rental price, $\frac{R}{P}$. The derivation of the *marginal product of capital* is similar to that of the MP_L from chapter 3.

4.2.2 Marginal Product of Capital

We begin with a Cobb–Douglas production function:

$$Y_t = A_t K_t^\alpha L_t^\beta$$

The marginal product of capital is defined as the additional output that a firm receives from the renting of an additional unit of capital, holding the level of technology and stock of labor constant.

$$MP_K = \frac{\Delta Y}{\Delta K} = F(K_t + 1, \bar{L}_t) - F(K_t, \bar{L}_t)$$

With regard to the general form of the Cobb–Douglas production function, we can calculate the marginal product of capital by taking the partial derivative of output with respect to capital:

$$MP_K = \alpha A_t K_t^{\alpha-1} L_t^\beta$$

this can be re-written as:

$$MP_K = \alpha\left(\frac{A_t K_t^\alpha L_t^\beta}{K}\right)$$

which simplifies to α multiplied by the average product of capital:

$$MP_K = \alpha\left(\frac{Y_t}{K_t}\right)$$

4.2.3 Rental Cost of Capital

When discussing the cost of capital, we must consider the rates of interest and depreciation. Assuming firms purchase capital with borrowed money, the firm will have to repay the loan with interest. If the firm chooses to use its *own* money to purchase capital, it forgoes the interest income it *would have* earned, had it purchased bonds instead.[2]

Every period, a percentage of capital *breaks down* due to use. *Depreciation* is understood to be the exogenous rate at which capital deteriorates, over time, due to normal *wear and tear*. This makes the nominal cost of capital

$$(r_t + \delta)P_K$$

where r is the real interest rate, the real cost of borrowing for the purchase of capital, and δ is the rate of depreciation.

The *real cost of capital* would therefore be expressed

$$(r_t + \delta)\frac{P_K}{P}$$

4.2.4 Profit Decisions

As previously stated, a firm's goal is to maximize profit. A firm's profit is equal to the difference between the real *rental* rate and the real *cost* of capital.

$$\text{Profit} = MP_K - (r_t + \delta)\frac{P_K}{P}$$

Given the diminishing nature of marginal products, the more capital increases, the smaller its marginal product. This means that if the firm is experiencing positive profit, the firm will increase the quantity of capital to increase profit; however, if the firm does *not* have positive profit, it is better to decrease the quantity of capital. The investment decision is therefore a function of profit.

---

[2]We discuss this more in chapter 6.

4.2.5   Investment Function

Firms must, in any time period, purchase new capital, not only on the basis of profit, but also to replace capital that has depreciated. Total, or *gross* business fixed investment is therefore a function of the marginal product of capital, the real interest rate, the rate of depreciation, and the real price of capital.

$$I_b = I_b(MP_K - (r_t + \delta)\tfrac{P_K}{P}) + \delta K_t$$

4.2.6   Residential Fixed Investment

The BEA defines *residential investment* as investment "in residential structures and equipment, primarily new construction of single-family and multifamily units." Spending on residential capital is dependent on the cost of borrowing (the real interest rate) and the relative price of housing. Anything that affects the demand for housing will affect residential investment. When the interest rate is low, there is an incentive to borrow more for the purposes of buying *new* units. Given that the *stock* of new units is fixed, at any given time, as the demand for housing increases, the relative price of housing increases. This increase in price signals that investment in housing will be more profitable, encouraging an increase residential investment to provide *new* units.

4.2.7   Inventory Investment

As firms make production decisions, throughout the business cycle, they are unaware of what demand changes may occur, in the market. Perhaps their production is in excess of what the market demands. This is known as unintended inventory investment. In this case, Y_t is greater than sales in time t. At the end of the year, inventory investment increases, allowing those goods to be available for sale in the future. At that future time, the firm is able to sell more units than it was able to produce, in that year, Y_{t+1}, causing inventory to fall.

Not all inventory investment is unintended. If a firm expects future sales to be higher and it wishes to *prepare*, it may overproduce in the current time period to *stockpile* goods for future sales.

In some cases, at the end of the year, firms have goods that have not been completed yet. *Works in progress* are counted as inventory, since they count as future output.

A firm's decision to hold inventory is dependent on the real interest rate. Since it costs money to store unsold product or works in progress, at higher interest rates, the firm is paying more for the inventory if it is financing through borrowing and forgoing the interest income by not holding bonds.

4.3   Government Expenditure

The government uses taxes and government expenditure to influence overall economic spending. Both government expenditure, $\bar{G}$, and tax revenue, $\bar{T}$, are believed to be exogenous, since the government sets its overall budget at the beginning of the fiscal year, laying-out how much it intends to raise in revenue and spend on goods, services, transfers, and projects.

4.3.1   Fiscal Policy

A nation chooses to utilize one of two types of *fiscal policy:*

- Expansionary, in which the government increases expenditure, $\uparrow G$, and/or decreases revenue, $\downarrow T$, in the hopes of stimulating the economy
- Contractionary, in which the government decreases expenditure, $\downarrow G$, and/or increases revenue, $\uparrow T$, to slowdown the economy

4.3.2   The Budget

A nation's government faces three possible spending situations:

1. Budget surplus: The case where a nation raises more in revenue than they intend to spend

$$\bar{T}_t > \bar{G}_t$$

2. Balanced budget: The case where revenue equals spending

$$\bar{T}_t = \bar{G}_t$$

3. Budget deficit: The case where spending is greater than revenue

$$\bar{T}_t < \bar{G}_t$$

Table 4.1: US government revenue/expenditure 2000–2017, billions $

	Revenues	Outlays	+/-
2000	2,025.2	1,789.0	236.2
2001	1,991.1	1,862.8	128.2
2002	1,853.1	2,010.9	-157.8
2003	1,782.3	2,159.9	-377.6
2004	1,880.1	2,292.8	-412.7
2005	2,153.6	2,472.0	-318.3
2006	2,406.9	2,655.1	-248.2
2007	2,568.0	2,728.7	-160.7
2008	2,524.0	2,982.5	-458.6
2009	2,105.0	3,517.7	-1,412.7
2010	2,162.7	3,457.1	-1,294.4
2011	2,303.5	3,603.1	-1,299.6
2012	2,450.0	3,536.9	-1,087.0
2013	2,775.1	3,454.6	-679.5
2014	3,021.5	3,506.1	-484.6
2015	3,249.9	3,688.4	-438.5
2016	3,268.0	3,852.6	-584.7
2017	3,316.2	3,981.6	-665.4

As we see, in table 4.1, the US has run a budget *deficit* every year since 2002. It is generally accepted that, in years when the economy *slows down*, the federal government will run a deficit to stimulate the economy. This is seen in the years beginning in 2008, in response to what economists called the *Great Recession*. In fiscal year 2017, US government *revenue* was roughly $3.3 trillion, with government *expenditure* roughly $4 trillion, giving the US a $665 billion budget deficit.

A budget deficit is believed to consist of a cyclical and structural component. The type of deficit spending that is done as a result of the normal workings of the business cycle is known as *cyclical* deficit spending. In a recession, unemployment is high; therefore, government expenditure cannot rely on income tax revenue as a source of revenue. This type of deficit spending does not concern economists, since it is believed that the deficit will be paid for when the economy recovers and experiences a budget surplus.

The *other* type of deficit spending that causes a bit more concern for economists, is *structural* deficit spending. This is the type of deficit spending that occurs as a result of general tax revenue being insufficient to finance government expenditure.

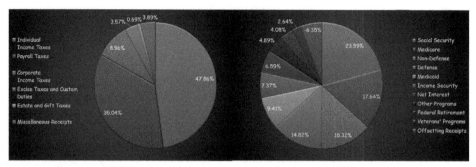

Figure 4.3: Sources and uses of government expenditure, 2017

Figure 4.3 shows that the largest sources of government revenue in 2017 are *individual income tax* and *payroll tax*, comprising over 80 percent of revenue; and the largest uses of spending are *Social Security*, *Medicare*, and *non-defense* spending, totaling approximately 57 percent.

4.3.3   Deficit versus Debt

One of the most common misconceptions in macroeconomics is confusing the government budget *deficit* and government *debt*. The deficit is, as previously stated, spending in excess of revenue, while government debt is the accumulation of multiple deficits over time.

If a nation begins a year, t, carrying debt from the previous year, $t - 1$, than the current year's expenditure is comprised of debt service and current deficit spending:

$$\text{Current Spending} = rD_{t-1} + G_t - T_t$$

where rD_{t-1} is the interest payments that must be made on last year's debt. Total debt *this year* is equal to the sum of last year's debt, the interest on last year's debt, and this year's deficit spending:

$$D_t = D_{t-1} + rD_{t-1} + G_t - T_t$$

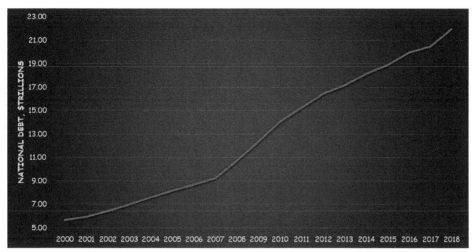

Figure 4.4: US public debt, 2000–2018, trillions

As figure 4.4 illustrates, US government debt grew steadily for the first seven years of the twenty-first century and began growing faster since the Great Recession. This is in-line with what we know about deficit spending.

4.3.4   Financing a Budget Deficit

In order to make-up for a shortfall in government revenue, the government generally issues bonds to finance the deficit. This *can*, as we will discuss in Chapter 7, lead to fiscal *crowding out*, in which increasing G leads to increasing interest rates, which discourages private investment. The government can also finance the spending by *creating* new money. As we will see in chapter 6, *seigniorage* can be used to finance spending when taxes cannot be raised; however, it does lead to monetary instability.

4.3.5   Taxes and the Ricardian Equivalence

The use of Expansionary fiscal policy to stimulate consumption expenditure is predicated on the belief that consumers will *respond* to changes in disposable income. What if a decrease in taxes did *not* stimulate an increase in consumption? This is the question raised by eighteenth century economist David Ricardo.

The *Ricardian equivalence* posits that, if a government utilizes deficit spending, consumers realize that, eventually, the government will have to repay the money, necessitating an increase in taxes in the future. In response to this, with a decrease in current taxes, consumers *save*, knowing that their taxes will eventually increase to pay down the debt. So, with an increase in disposable income, consumers do not increase spending, but rather, *save* the tax cut, undermining the expansionary effect of the policy.

4.4 Savings

Whenever an economic agent forgoes current consumption for *future* consumption, savings are created. There are three types of savings that need to be dealt with:

1. Savings by consumers
   Total income of consumers minus consumption spending, personal interest payments, personal transfer payments and tax payments

2. Savings by firms
   Total profit of firms minus depreciation, dividend payments, and corporate taxes

3. Savings by government
   Total government revenue minus total government expenditures

4.4.1 National Savings (S_t)

National savings, sometimes called *net savings*, equals the sum of personal savings, undistributed corporate profits, and net government savings.

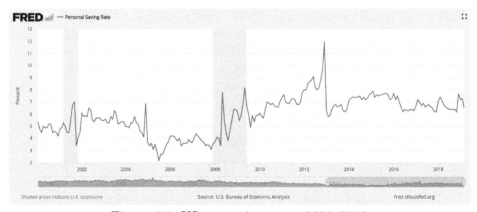

Figure 4.5: US net savings rate, 2000–2018

Another way to look at national savings is national income minus consumption and government spending. Since we know that output is a function of capital and labor, consumption is a function of disposable income, and government spending is exogenous, we can define national savings as

$$\bar{S}_t = \bar{Y}_t(\bar{A}_t, \bar{K}_t, \bar{L}_t) - \bar{C}_t(\bar{Y}_t - \bar{T}_t) - \bar{G}_t$$

If there is an *increase* in national income, *increases* in taxes, and/or *decreases* in government spending, national savings will increase. If national income *decreases*, taxes *increase*, and/or government spending *decreases*, we expect an *increase* in national savings.

What Changes	Effect on Savings
Y_t increases T_t increases G_t decreases	S_t *increases*
Y_t decreases T_t decreases G_t increases	S_t *decreases*

Since none of the determinants of national savings are believed to be influenced by changes in the real interest rate, national savings is believed to be perfectly price inelastic, with regard to r, represented by a vertical line.[3]

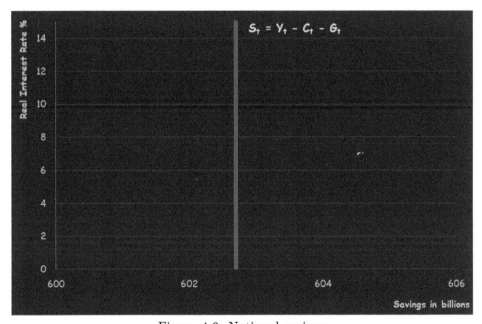

Figure 4.6: National savings

---

[3]We relax this assumption in section 7 of this chapter.

4.5   Goods Market Equilibrium

In a closed economy, the goods market is said to be in equilibrium when the price level is such that total or *aggregate* supply of domestic goods (Y_t) is equal to the total or *aggregate* demand for domestic goods ($C_t + I_t + G_t$).

As we saw, the supply of all goods in the economy is a function of the level of technology available in the economy, as well as the stock of labor and capital. Since we assume that, in the long run, the economy will be functioning at full employment, we feel safe assuming that the full-employment level of output (Y_t^*) can be calculated and is known.

Since consumption, according to Keynes, is a function of disposable income, both parts of which we know, we feel safe assuming that the level of consumption spending is also known. Government spending, being decided by the government, is assumed exogenous, meaning that we take it as *given*. Bearing all these assumptions in mind, we can rewrite the goods market equilibrium as

$$Y_t^* = \bar{C}_t + I_t(r_t) + \bar{G}_t$$

4.5.1   Importance of the Real Interest Rate

As we see, in a closed economy, in the long run, if the level of aggregate expenditure is *not* equal to the full-employment level of GDP, the equilibriating factor is investment. We assume that the real interest rate will adjust to equate GDP and aggregate spending.

If $Y_t^* < \bar{C}_t + I_t(r_t) + \bar{G}_t$, it means that the real interest rate will increase, discouraging investment; while, if $Y_t^* > \bar{C}_t + I_t(r_t) + \bar{G}_t$, the real interest rate will fall, increasing investment and bringing the market into equilibrium.

4.5.2   Savings and Investment

The reason we believe the real interest rate will adjust, equilibriating the market for goods, comes from the unique relationship that exists between national savings and investment, in the *market for loanable funds*. In this market, the *supply* of loanable funds is represented by national savings, and *demand* is represented by investment.

National savings in a closed economy, as we stated earlier, is equal to national income minus consumption and government spending.

$$\bar{S}_t = \bar{Y}_t - \bar{C}_t - \bar{G}_t$$

Investment, according to Keynes, is negatively related to the real interest rate. To see this, let's return to the model for business fixed investment, in which increases in r, holding everything else constant, increases the real cost of capital and decreases profit. So, at higher levels of r, the quantity of investment demanded decreases.

$$I_b = I_b(MP_K - (r_t + \delta)\frac{P_K}{P}) + \delta K_t$$

4.5.3   Shifts in Investment

Any change to MP_K or $\frac{P_K}{P}$ affects profit and therefore shifts investment demand. Assuming that savings is fixed, any increase in investment causes a *fall* in the real interest rate. The marginal product of capital increases with technological progress, which increases productivity, increases the demand for investment, shifting the curve to the right. Decreases in net corporate taxes cause decreases in the price of capital, leading to an increase in profit, which increases investment demand, shifting it to the right.

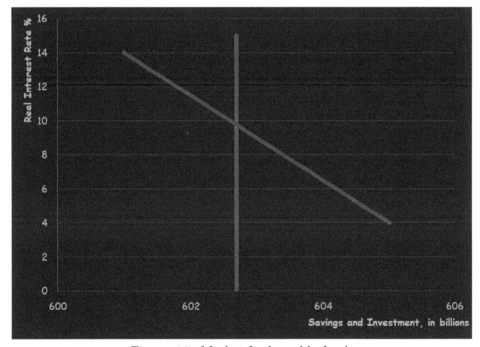

Figure 4.7: Market for loanable funds

Since the supply of loanable funds is fixed, shifts in investment demand change the real interest rate. The real interest rate will adjust to equilibriate savings and investment.

Since $\bar{S}_t = \bar{Y}_t - \bar{C}_t - \bar{G}_t$, when the market for loanable funds is in equilibrium,

$$\bar{S}_t = I_t(r_t{}^*)$$
$$\bar{Y}_t - \bar{C}_t - \bar{G}_t = I_t(r_t{}^*)$$

which re-arranges to:

$$\bar{Y}_t = \bar{C}_t + I_t(r_t{}^*) + \bar{G}_t$$

In other words, when we have equilibrium in the market for loanable funds, we simultaneously have equilibrium in the market for goods.

4.6   Alternative Consumption Theories

While income is a major influence on consumption, there is *more* to the consumption decision than Keynes realized in 1936. We will look at a few of the alternative models of consumption that have been developed out of *intertemporal* choice.

4.6.1   Irving Fisher and Intertemporal Consumption

Unlike Keynes, Irving Fisher believes that consumption decisions are made, not based on current income, but with the goal of maximizing lifetime utility, which requires the consumer to pay attention to interest rates.

Fisher's book *Theory of Interest*,[4] introduces the idea that, if a consumer has the ability to borrow against future income, he or she faces an *intertemporal budget constraint*. In this case, consumption is dependent on not only income, but also the real interest rate.

This budget constraint is defined as

$$C_1 + \frac{C_2}{1+r} = Y_1 + \frac{Y_2}{1+r}$$

where current consumption and future consumption (which is discounted, based on the interest rate) equal to lifetime income.

So, the problem that the typical consumer faces is maximizing lifetime utility, subject to a lifetime budget constraint. Whether the consumer *forgoes* current consumption for *future* consumption (saving) or forgoes future consumption for *current* (dissaving) depends on his or her preferences.

---

[4]Irving Fisher, *Theory of Interest* (New York: The Macmillan Company, 1930).

4.6.2 Life–Cycle Hypothesis

In 1966, Franco Modigliani first published his life-cycle hypothesis,[5] in which he posits that households make consumption decisions, not based on *current* disposable income, but based on the resources they will have in the lifetime of the household. By making decisions in this way, consumers are able to *smooth* their consumption, over their lifetime. In other words, while consumers are participating in the labor force, they are saving a portion of their income to sustain them in the years when they are no longer earning labor income. If this is true, consumers equally divide their *resources* over all the years of their life.

For the purposes of this example, let us assume that we are talking about a typical consumer. This consumer begins with an initial level of wealth, W. Every year of employment, the consumer earns a fixed income, Y, and the consumer intends to work for a known number of years, R, and believes that he or she has T years of life to live. That means that the consumption function for the individual equally divides the resources, for the life of the consumer.

$$C_t = \frac{(W + RY)}{T}$$

This function can be rewritten:

$$C_t = \alpha W + \beta Y$$

where α and β reflect consumption's sensitivity to changes in wealth and income, respectively.

Several issues are raised by the life-cycle hypothesis including the assumption that consumers know (a) how many years they will work, (b) what their state of health will be all the years of their life, and (c) how much will be required to pay for any *unexpected* expenses that may arise.

4.6.3 Permanent Income Hypothesis

Developed by Milton Friedman in the 1950s, the permanent income hypothesis[6] also assumes that consumers are attempting to smooth consumption over their lifetime; however, the definition of income differs.

Friedman believes that consumption is a function of both present and expected future income. Current income is made up of permanent and transitory income, such that

---

[5]"The Life Cycle Hypothesis of Saving, the Demand for Wealth and the Supply of Capital" *Social Research* 33, no. 2 (1966): 160–217.

[6]"The Permanent Income Hypothesis," *A Theory of the Consumption Function.* (Princeton, NJ: Princeton University Press, 1957): 20–37.

$$Y_t = Y^p + Y^t$$

Permanent income is income that the households expect to receive, while transitory income is any unexpected increase or decrease in income that may occur. Since Y^p is expected, consumers change their savings decisions to adjust to random transitory changes in income.

Since all consumption is dependent on current income and the consumer believes that only *permanent* income is assured, consumption is dependent, mostly, on permanent income. The consumption function, given the permanent income hypothesis, therefore, is

$$C_t = \alpha Y^p$$

where α is the proportion of permanent income that consumers spend.

4.6.4   Random Walk Hypothesis

Robert Hall[7] takes Friedman's theory of permanent income and adds consumers' expectations about future income.

Beginning from the assumption that consumers utilize all available information when making decisions about the future, Hall finds that the *only* changes in consumption spending are due to unexpected changes in wealth or income. If this is true, consumption spending is expected to follow a *random walk* process, making the prediction of future consumption expenditure impossible.

4.7   Alternative Savings Theories

We have, up until now, assumed that the savings decision is done regardless of the real interest rate. We based our discussion of the market for loanable funds on a fixed supply of savings; however, what would happen if savings were affected by changes in r? With an intertemporal budget constraint, we can look at the potential incentives afforded the consumer by changes in the real interest rate. If consumers are borrowing in order to finance current consumption (e.g., mortgage, car loan), increases in the real interest rate punish the consumer for current consumption. An increase in the real interest rate gives consumers an incentive to save *now*, forgoing current consumption until the future.

---

[7]Robert Hall, "Stochastic Implications of the Life Cycle-Permanent Income Hypothesis: Theory and Evidence." *Journal of Political Economy* 86, no. 6 (Dec. 1978) 971–987

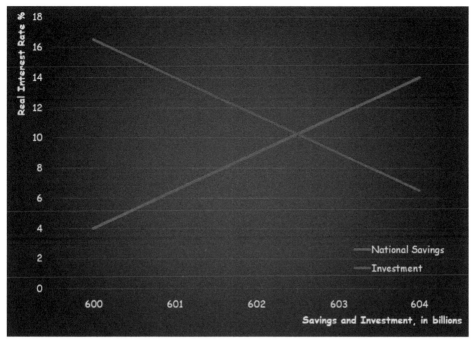

Figure 4.8: Market for loanable funds with S(r)

Food for Thought

1. *Fiscal crowding out:*

   ■ What happens to r_t when G_t increases?

   ■ How does this affect I_t?

   ■ How is this expected to affect aggregate expenditure?

2. *National income:*

   ■ Using the data source of your choice, what is consumption spending?

   ■ Investment?

   ■ Government?

   ■ What is the current level of the US deficit?

   ■ What is national savings, currently?

3. *Hauser's law:*

- *Google* "Hauser's law"
- What is it?
- Do you feel it makes sense?

Chapter 5

Long-Run Economic Growth

> In any given moment we have two
> options: to step forward into
> growth or to step back into safety.
>
> ―――――――――――――
>
> Alexander Maslow

Before we can begin a discussion of the mechanics of economic growth, it is important to dispel a common misconception.

Many people look to *any* increase in GDP that a nation experiences and call it growth. This is not the case.

In any given period of time, GDP can increase for a number of different reasons. As we saw, in chapter 2, nominal GDP can increase due to increases in price levels. We also see increases in GDP (both nominal and real) when the economy is in the recovery stage of its business cycle,[1] after a recession.

Economic *growth* can be defined as an increase in the productive capacity of a nation. This can be seen as increases in the full-employment level of output, also referred to as *potential* GDP. As we have previously discussed, full-employment GDP (Y_t^*) is a function of the technology, capital, and labor that the nation has at its disposal.

$$Y_t^* = F(\bar{A}_t, \bar{K}_t, \bar{L}_t^*)$$

For us to discuss growth, we must consider how and why changes in these factors are responsible for changes in Y_t^*, as well as what policies can be utilized to encourage (or discourage) continued growth.

―――――――――――――――――――――

[1]We will discuss the business cycle in detail in chapter 9.

61

$$\Delta Y^* = Y^*_{t+1} - Y^*_t$$

Understanding this can help explain why some nations grow faster than others while others do not grow at all. In measuring growth, we have to ask, "Is it enough that Y^*_t increases, or do we have to concern ourselves with improvements in the overall *well-being* of the people of the nation?" Discussions of *economic growth versus economic development* are many and larger than the scope of this chapter. For ease of analysis, let us accept the common measure of growth of *real GDP*.

Table 5.1: Selected 2017 Real GDP growth rates[2]

United States	2.2
China	6.9
Germany	2.5
Italy	1.5
Japan	1.7
Philippines	6.7
Puerto Rico	-2.4
South Africa	1.3
Venezuela	-14

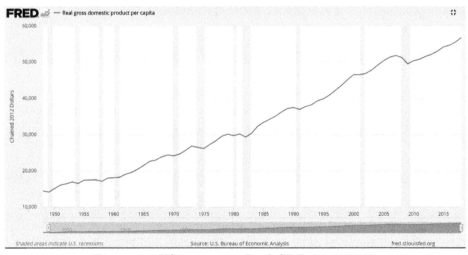

Figure 5.1 US per-capita Real GDP, 1948–2018

[2]CIA World Factbook, "GDP - Real Growth Rate",
https://www.cia.gov/library/publications/the-world-factbook/fields/210rank.html

5.1   Classical Growth

In what has come to be known as *classical growth theory*, technological progress is assumed constant, and since output is agreed to be a product of factors whose increasing use experiences diminishing returns, it is believed that, at some point, the return on the factor will be zero. In his 1798 *An Essay on the Principle of Population*,[3] Thomas Malthus discusses how increases in population affect the overall well-being of the people, finding that increases in per-capita GDP are short lived.

To understand Malthus, one must consider the *subsistence* level, a standard of living that offers *only* the bare necessities of life. If people have the minimum necessary to survive, population growth is expected to be low, given that there is no incentive to have children. *Any* increase in standard of living gives households an incentive to increase population. When population increases, as we saw in chapter 3, labor productivity increases, which increases GDP; however, given that population grows faster than labor productivity, the per-capita GDP returns to the subsistence level, preventing society from *ever* experiencing prosperity.

Malthusians often speak of the forces that keep population in *check*. *Positive* checks to population include anything that increases the death rate (e.g., war, famine, pestilence), while *preventative* checks, or moral restraints, include any force that decreases the birth rate (e.g., celibacy, selective breeding.) To this end, classical growth theorists believe increases in per-capita GDP are temporary, leading to temporary increases in the population growth rate, which lead to decreases in per-capita GDP.

5.2   Neo-Classical Growth

Developed in 1956, simultaneously, by Robert Solow and Trevor Swan, the *neo-classical growth theory* relates how long-run economic growth is affected by a nation's savings, population growth, and the growth rate of technological progress.

5.2.1   Solow–Swan Model

Since we are measuring growth using per-capita GDP, it will simplify things to consider the economy in *per unit of labor* terms, as per-capita. We begin by looking at the Cobb–Douglas production function, which exhibits constant returns, and aggregate expenditure, ignoring government spending, for the time being.

---

[3]Thomas R. Malthus and Anthony Flew, *An Essay on the Principle of Population: and, A Summary View of the Principle of Population; Edited with an Introduction by Anthony Flew.* Harmondsworth: Penguin, 1982.

$$
\begin{aligned}
Y_t &= F(K_t, L_t) = K_t^\alpha L_t^{1-\alpha} \\
Y_t &= C_t + I_t
\end{aligned}
$$

We can divide through by L to find that per-capita output is a function of capital stock per worker and equal to consumption and investment spending per capita. It is customary to use lower case letters to denote per-capita terms in this model.

$$
\frac{Y_t}{L_t} = F\left(\frac{K_t}{L_t}, \frac{L_t}{L_t}\right)
$$

$$
\begin{aligned}
y_t &= f(k_t, 1) \\
&= f(k_t) = k_t^\alpha
\end{aligned}
$$

$$
y_t = c_t + i_t
$$

where per-capita consumption is based on income not saved, and per-capita investment is dependent on savings. In this simplified model, with the absence of government spending, the savings decision is based *only* on consumption.

$$
\begin{aligned}
c_t &= (1-s)y_t \\
&= (1-s)f(k_t) \\
&= (1-s)k_t^\alpha
\end{aligned}
$$

$$
\begin{aligned}
i_t &= sy_t \\
&= sf(k_t) \\
&= sk_t^\alpha
\end{aligned}
$$

5.2.2   Growth: This Is How We Do It

If per-capita output is a function of per-capita capital stock, as k increases, y increases. Since aggregate production experiences diminishing returns, as k increases, y increases at a decreasing rate.

The key to growth, according to neo-classical theory, lies in the *accumulation* of capital. Capital stock increases with investment and, as we learned in chapter 4, decreases due to depreciation. The rate of per-capita investment, in a given time period, i_t, is dependent on the rate of savings, s, while the rate of depreciation, as previously stated, is exogenous and denoted by δ. In order for per-capita output to increase in the future, current investment in capital is vital, so as to replace the capital, which depreciated in the previous period. Based on this, and assuming that the labor force is not growing, we can define the *change* in per-capita capital stock as

$$
\begin{aligned}
k_{t+1} - k_t &= \Delta k \\
\Delta k &= sk_t^\alpha - \delta k_t
\end{aligned}
$$

As we saw in chapter 3, anything that increases the amount of labor that is supplied in the market will increase *potential* GDP. Unlike the classical economists, the neo-classical theory believes that population grows independent of GDP. It is assumed that the labor force will grow, as the population grows, at the exogenous rate, n. As with depreciation, changes in the labor force affect per-capita capital stock. As the labor force increases, there *must* be investment in capital, to prevent per-capita capital stock from decreasing. Assuming no depreciation, the change in per-capita capital stock would be:

$$\Delta k \quad = sk_t^\alpha - nk_t$$

Accounting for both *depreciation* and *population growth*, the formula for capital accumulation, known as Solow's *law of motion of capital*, can be rewritten:

$$\Delta k \quad = sk_t^\alpha - (\delta + n)k_t$$

where $(\delta + n)k_t$ is the per-capita investment required to make up for capital that has worn-out and new workers, entering the labor force, who require capital.

There are three possible situations with this equation. Per-capita capital stock will be increasing, if investment *exceeds* the required level; decreasing, if investment is below the required level; or remain unchanged if investment is equal to the required level. Per-capita output, as well as per-capita consumption, depends on which it is.

	Δk	Δy
$sk_t^\alpha > (\delta + n)k_t$	↑	↑
$sk_t^\alpha = (\delta + n)k_t$	no change	no change
$sk_t^\alpha < (\delta + n)k_t$	↓	↓

5.2.3   Reaching the Steady State

The *steady state* is the level of per-capita capital stock, k^*, at which $\Delta k = 0$. If the initial allocation of capital stock is *below* k^*, capital will accumulate, due to investment being above the required level, and the economy will grow. Notice that it does not matter what the initial allocation of capital stock happens to be. Wherever the economy starts, it will grow toward its steady state. Once at its steady state, both k and y are constant.

The steady state is found by solving Solow's law of motion for k^*:

$$sk_t^{*\alpha} \quad = (\delta + n)k_t^*$$

$$k^* \quad = \left(\frac{s}{\delta + n}\right)^{\frac{1}{1-\alpha}}$$

Once we know the value of k^*, we can use it to calculate y^* & c^*:

$$y^* = \quad k^{*\alpha} \quad = \left(\frac{s}{\delta+n}\right)^{\frac{\alpha}{1-\alpha}}$$

$$c^* = \quad (1-s)y^* \quad = \left(1-s\right)\left(\frac{s}{\delta+n}\right)^{\frac{\alpha}{1-\alpha}}$$

It is important to note that every nation accumulates capital to reach its *own* steady state. Since capital accumulation is, in part, due to the capital *leftover* from the previous period, the smaller the initial allocation of k and the further away from the steady state, the faster the nation will accumulate capital. The *rate* at which the economy will grow toward its steady state can be calculated by dividing both sides of the law of motion by k_t:

$$\frac{\Delta k}{k} = \frac{s}{k_t^{1-\alpha}} - (\delta+n)$$

When in its steady state, $k_t = k^*$, a nation will no longer accumulate capital, since the distance from the steady state is zero, $\frac{\Delta k}{k_t} = 0$. It is worth noting that while k and y are constant in the steady state, since the labor force is assumed to grow at a rate of n, in the steady state, real GDP, Y, will also grow at a rate of n.

There are *two* kinds of people, in the world: people who process information mathematically and those who like pretty pictures. In order for us to *see* the dynamics of the Solow–Swan model, let us examine a mathematical example with pictures.

5.2.4   A Mathe*Magical* Example

It is safe to assume that capital depreciates at the same exogenous rate, in every country; however, a nation's savings and population growth rates may differ. Let us assume that there is a nation, which we will call Mullog. In the baseline case, the following conditions exist:

α	0.50
s	0.30
n	0.05
δ	0.10

Mullog's per-capita output is seen, in figure 5.2, to increase as we increase the quantity of capital stock per worker; and exhibits diminishing marginal product of capital, MPK, reflected by the slope of the line. Graphically speaking, as capital stock per worker increases, the line gets *flatter*.

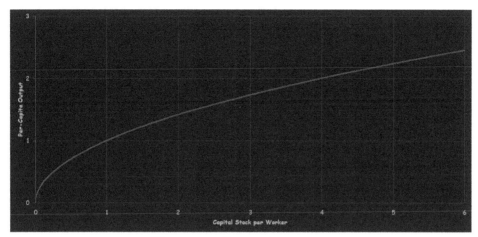

Figure 5.2: Per-capita output

Figure 5.3 shows the per-capita investment (blue) and required investment (green) curves, graphically revealing the steady state level of capital stock per worker.

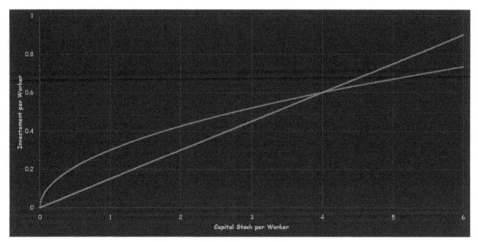

Figure 5.3: The steady state

Mullog's steady state levels of capital stock, income, and consumption per capita are calculated to be

$$k^* = \left(\frac{0.30}{0.10 + 0.05}\right)^{\frac{1}{1-0.5}}$$
$$= 4.0$$

$$y^* = 4.0^{0.5}$$
$$= 2.0$$

$$
\begin{aligned}
c^* &= (1 - 0.30)2.0 \\
&= 1.4
\end{aligned}
$$

According to the model, savings is the determining factor in investment. If the nation's savings rate increases, investment increases, leading the nation to experience increases in steady state levels of both per-capita income and consumption. This also means that, according to the model, nations with higher savings rates will have higher levels of per-capita capital stock which leads to higher per-capita income and consumption. Both table 5.2 and figure 5.4 show how, with increasing levels of savings, nations end up with higher steady state levels of capital stock per worker.

Table 5.2: Effects of Δs on steady state

	k^*	y^*	c^*
$s = 0.3$	4.0	2.0	1.4
$s = 0.4$	$7.\overline{111}$	$2.\overline{666}$	1.6
$s = 0.5$	$11.\overline{111}$	$3.\overline{333}$	$1.\overline{666}$

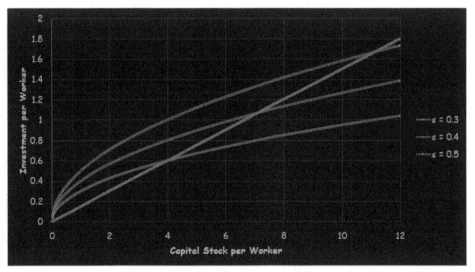

Figure 5.4: Steady state as s changes

If the nation's population growth rate increases, more workers need to be equipped with capital. With more workers, there is less capital stock to replace depreciation. In order to maintain our level of output per worker, the required rate of investment must increase, leading to a lower steady state level of per-capita capital stock. This means that nations with higher population growth rates will have lower steady states, leading to lower levels of per-capita income and consumption. Both table 5.3 and figure 5.5 show how, as the population growth rate increases, nations end up growing to lower steady state levels of capital stock per worker.

Table 5.3: Effects of Δn on steady state

	k^*	y^*	c^*
$n = 0.05$	4.0	2.0	1.4
$n = 0.10$	2.25	1.5	1.05
$n = 0.15$	1.44	1.2	0.84
$n = 0.20$	1.0	1.0	0.70

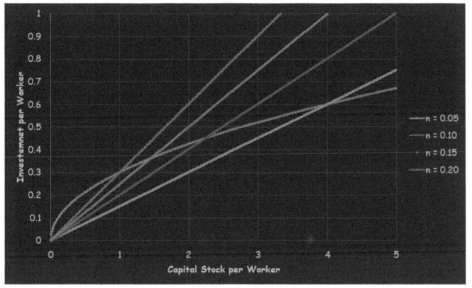

Figure 5.5: Steady state as n changes

For completeness sake, let us, for a moment, look at what happens when capital's contribution to the productive process changes. The larger α, the smaller the diminishing returns. If diminishing returns are less of a force against accumulation of capital, the steady state level of capital per worker increases.

Table 5.4: Effects of $\Delta \alpha$ on steady state

	k^*	y^*	c^*
$\alpha = 0.5$	4.0	2.0	1.4
$\alpha = 0.6$	5.657	2.378	1.665
$\alpha = 0.7$	10.079	3.175	2.222
$\alpha = 0.8$	32	5.657	3.960

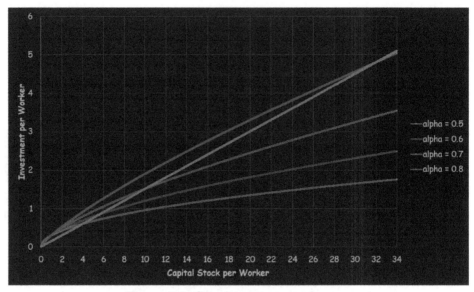

Figure 5.6: Steady state as α changes

5.2.5   Analysis of the Solow Growth Model

Since nations grow to their *own* steady state, and given that a nation's steady state is determined by s, n, and α, one can only accurately compare nations whose rate of savings and population growth are the same. Assuming that Mullog's neighboring country, Noruas, faces the same production function and has the same rate of savings and population growth rate, the model predicts that both nations will *grow* to the same steady state. If Noraus starts with a lower level of initial capital stock per worker, it is predicted that it will have lower per-capita GDP, and will, therefore, be *poorer* than in relation to Mullog, starting further away from the steady state. Since the further away from its steady state the faster a nation grows, Noraus is predicted to grow *faster* than Mullog.

Generally speaking, nations with higher per-capita GDP *tend* to have *higher* savings rates and *lower* population growth rates and capital's share of production tends to be *larger*. However, assuming that Mullog's *other* neighbor, Rodrom, faces the same production function, has a lower rate of savings, and has a higher population growth rate, the model predicts it will have a *lower* steady state, therefore leading to lower per-capita GDP.

5.2.6 Total Factor Productivity (A)

Not all changes in output are explained by changes in the *quantity* of capital and labor inputs used in production. When discussing Δy, we must consider how efficiently the inputs are used. Total factor productivity accounts for the effects of technological progress. We denote technological progress as being *labor augmenting* and rewrite the production function to account for it, where A_t is the level of technology:

$$Y_t = F(K_t, A_t L_t)$$

Technological progress is seen when A increases, at what is assumed to be an exogenous rate, g, over time. As technology increases, labor becomes more productive, so at higher values of A, we expect higher levels of output.

The only difference this makes *ideologically* is that y is now looked on as output per unit of *effective* or augmented labor. Model-wise, this introduces a new force that affects required investment. Where previously we were only concerned with replacing capital that had worn out and equipping laborers new to the labor force, now we must also account for acquiring capital for more productive laborers.

The law of motion and all of the previous formulae are rewritten:

$$\Delta k = sk_t^\alpha - (\delta + n + g)k_t$$

$$sk_t^{*\alpha} = (\delta + n + g)k_t^*$$

$$k^* = \left(\frac{s}{\delta + n + g}\right)^{\frac{1}{1-\alpha}}$$

$$y^* = \left(\frac{s}{\delta + n + g}\right)^{\frac{\alpha}{1-\alpha}}$$

$$c^* = \left(1 - s\right)\left(\frac{s}{\delta + n + g}\right)^{\frac{\alpha}{1-\alpha}}$$

Yet again, in the steady state, k is constant; however, now that labor is growing at rate n and becoming more efficient at a rate of g, at the steady state, the level of output per worker is growing at a rate of g and real GDP is growing at a rate of $n + g$.

These cosmetic differences in the model still show that the key to growth is capital accumulation, and since *that* is dependent on savings, and different rates of savings lead to different steady states, we must look at how a nation *knows* which s is best.

5.2.7   The Golden Rule

The goals of economic growth *should* include increasing the overall well-being of the population. In his 1966 book,[4] Edmund Phelps speaks about the optimal level of savings. By *optimal*, s must lie between 0 and 1. If a nation finds itself in a steady state for which $s = 0$, 100 percent of income is consumed, with no investment in capital. This would all but stop growth with k^*, y^* & c^* all equal to 0.

$$k^* \quad = \left(\frac{0}{\delta + n + g} \right)^{\frac{1}{1-\alpha}} \qquad = 0$$

$$y^* \quad = \left(\frac{0}{\delta + n + g} \right)^{\frac{\alpha}{1-\alpha}} \qquad = 0$$

$$c^* \quad = \left(1 - 0 \right) \left(\frac{0}{\delta + n + g} \right)^{\frac{\alpha}{1-\alpha}} \quad = 0$$

While a savings rate of 0 percent fails to maximize consumption, it turns out that it has the same affect on consumption as a savings rate of 100 percent. While a savings rate of 100 percent would maximize y, it leaves consumers no income for consumption.[5]

$$c^* \quad = \left(1 - 1 \right) \left(\frac{1}{\delta + n + g} \right)^{\frac{\alpha}{1-\alpha}} \quad = 0$$

We must find a steady state level of capital stock per worker, such that consumption is maximized. For the purposes of our analysis, we will look at maximizing per-capita consumption in the steady state, c^*_{gold}. If we maximize per-capita consumption, by extension we are maximizing aggregate consumption. Based on our previous discussion, aggregate consumption is maximized at the steady state where the difference between y and i is greatest.

---

[4]Edmund S. Phelps, *Golden Rules of Economic Growth: Studies of Efficient and Optimal Investment* (New York: Norton, 1969).

[5]The difference between "All you *can* eat" and "All you *care* to enjoy."

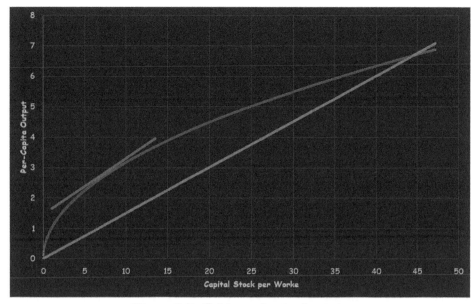

Figure 5.7: Golden rule steady state

Graphically, this is seen at the steady state, k_{gold}, at which the distance between y and the required investment line is greatest. In figure 5.7, it can be seen that the distance is greatest when the slope of y is equal to the slope of the required investment line. With this, we arrive at the general rule:

$$MP_K = \delta + n + g$$

Ideally, we want a nation to choose the steady state at which consumption is maximized; however, the economy does not necessarily *want* to be at the golden rule level of savings. This sometimes requires intervention on the part of the government.

5.3   Endogenous Growth

As we have seen, in the neo-classical model the long-run rate of growth is determined by either the savings rate or the rate of technical progress, both of which are exogenous. *Endogenous* growth theory, sometimes called *new growth theory*, recognizes the importance of the development of new technologies and the improvement of human capital.

5.3.1 AK Model

In endogenous growth theory, growth emanates from some *internal* cause. A simple example of endogenous growth stems from the assumption of a production function with constant returns to scale. Popularized by Paul Romer[6] in 1986, the model is based on the assumption that the production function does not experience diminishing returns to capital.[7] If true, the Cobb–Douglas production function can be re-written:

$$Y = AK$$

where A is total factor productivity and K is both physical *and* human capital.

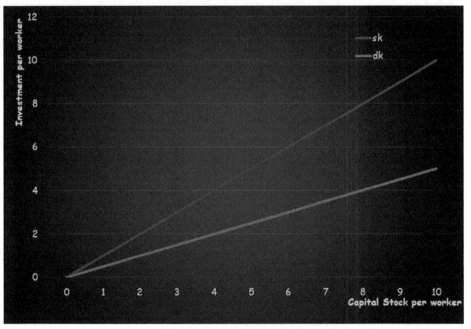

Figure 5.8: AK Model

If we take a simple case with no population growth, figure 5.8 gives us the AK[8] model where *dk* represents the investment per worker required to make up for capital that has worn-out due to depreciation, and *sk* represents investment per worker.

---

[6]Paul M. Romer, "Increasing Returns and Long-Run Growth," *Journal of Political Economy* 94, no. 5 (1986): 1002—1037.

[7]If the return to capital is *constant* $\alpha = 1$.

[8]The first AK models were introduced by Roy Harrod and Evsey Domar in the early 20th century.

Since investment is *always* greater than depreciation, the economy experiences growth that is never-ending. If true, any government policy that increases the rate of investment will *permanently* increase the growth rate.

5.3.2   Spillover Model

Previously we considered the case in which the production process experiences constant returns If we allow that productivity may *increase* due to positive externalities[9], or spillover, resulting from the accumulation of *knowledge*,[10] the production function can exhibit *increasing* returns.

Let us call η the effect of the positive knowledge externality and relax the assumption of constant returns. The AK model can now be written as:

$$Y = AK^{\alpha+\eta}$$

There are three possible situations:

1. $\alpha + \eta = 1$
   The knowledge spillover perfectly counters the decreasing returns to capital, leaving us with the AK model from the last section.

2. $\alpha + \eta < 1$
   The knowledge spillover is not enough to counter the effects of the decreasing returns, leaving us with a situation, not unlike the basic Solow model if there were no population growth or technological progress.[11]

3. $\alpha + \eta > 1$
   The knowledge spillover is large enough that the economy experiences never-ending growth. The difference between this and the case from the last section is that it is possible, in this situation, for the economy to experience what Charles Jones calls *explosive growth*[12] in which the growth rate increases at an ever-increasing rate.

---

[9]the benefit experienced by *one* economic agent, attributed to the cost to some *other* economic agent (e.g., the development of a new technology benefits everyone, not just the firm who spent the money to develop it.)

[10]Kenneth J. Arrow, "Economic Welfare and the Allocation of Resources for Invention," in *The Rate and Direction of Inventive Activity: Economic and Social Factors* (Princeton, NJ: Princeton University Press, 1962): 609-626.

[11]$(n + g) = 0$

[12]Charles I. Jones, "Growth: With or Without Scale Effects?," *American Economic Review Papers and Proceedings* 89, no. 2 (May 1999): 139-144.

5.4   Incentivizing Savings and Investment

Given the importance of savings and investment to neo-classical growth theory, one must ask what policies best influence these determinants of growth.

5.4.1   Savings

So much of what the government does potentially affects the rate of savings. As discussed in chapter 4, any policy that affects public or private saving will shift the supply of loanable funds, leading to changes in the real interest rate, which will affect investment.

$$\bar{S}_t = \bar{Y}_t - \bar{C}_t(\bar{Y}_t - \bar{T}_t) - \bar{G}_t$$

Fiscal policy, which we will discuss in more detail in chapter 10, involves changes to government spending and taxes. Fiscal policy can be used to give consumers and firms incentives to make different savings decisions; this is accomplished by either general or specific taxation. If the government utilizes general *expansionary* fiscal policy, increasing G and/or decreasing T, this is expected to lead to a *decrease* in net savings, which will lead to an increase in the real interest rate, leading to a decrease in investment. Likewise, *contractionary* fiscal policy, decreasing G and/or increasing T, will lead to *increases* in net savings, which leads to a decrease in the real interest rate, increasing investment.

The government can incentivize saving by offering specific tax *breaks* to individuals and firms who save. These *saver's credits* make certain retirement saving tax exempt, meaning that savers get to keep more of the interest they earn on savings instrument (e.g., Roth IRAs).

As we discussed in chapter 4, if saving is affected by changes in the real interest rate, *monetary policy*, changes to the money supply, as we will discuss in the next chapter, can be used to affect the interest rate, giving consumers and firms incentives to make different saving decisions. At *higher* interest rates, consumers and firms earn a higher return on their savings, which incentivizes saving.

Fiscal policy and monetary policy can also be used to affect investment decisions, which affects the productivity of labor, increasing the growth rate of technological progress.

5.4.2   Investment

When discussing investment decisions that affect growth, there are a number of ways that investment is significant. In his 2004 book,[13] William Bernstein writes of the four pillars of growth:

■ **Clearly defined property rights**
   When we discuss *property rights*, we are talking about the right of owner-ship, which entails, not only the right to *use* the good, but also *earn income* generated from ownership.

   If I rent a two-bedroom apartment for $600 a month, I am limited as to what I am allowed to do. If I am certain that the market value of the apart-ment is $2,000, I cannot advertise for a roommate and charge them $1,000 rent for the use of half of the apartment. Since I do not *own* the apartment, I cannot use the apartment to generate income. If I wish to generate income from the ownership of property, I have an incentive to buy property.

   The development of new technologies, production processes, or products increases productivity. Firms need incentives to invest in development. The firm wants to know that it will benefit from anything that it invents/discovers. In this way, the government providing/enforcing ownership incentivizes the firm to invest (e.g., copyrights, intellectual property rights, patents).

■ **Encouraging scientific reason**
   Since the economy can benefit from new processes, the government can directly conduct/finance research, hiring scientists, to study issues it feels will benefit the well-being of the economy, (e.g., National Aeronautics and Space Administration) or subsidize research through the issue of grants.

■ **Well-established capital markets**
   If it is believed that the open market will efficiently allocate productive resources toward the projects that will be the most socially beneficial the government should take whatever practicable means to improve the func-tioning of the market.

■ **Transportation/communication networks**
   Since the creation of new technologies can be sped-up through collabora-tion, the government can encourage development through making it easier for information and products to flow. Whether this entails investment in infrastructure or telecommunications, the government can increase the pro-ductive efficiency of the economy through directed spending.

---

[13]William J. Bernstein, *The Birth of Plenty* (New York: McGraw-Hill, 2004).

In addition to Bernstein's ideas on growth, rather than the government focusing on changes in capital, it could also increase growth through investment in labor. Two investments that can increase productivity of labor are education and health care.

■ **Human capital**

In chapter 3, we introduced the idea of *human capital,* the education, training, experience, and skill set of the labor force. As human capital grows, it is expected that productivity and wages will increase, leading to an increase in GDP. As US Federal Reserve Chair Jerome Powell stated in July of 2019,[14] "the education system needs to produce people who can take advantage of advancing technology and globalization." If the government wants to stimulate growth of human capital, it can invest in education. As seen in figure 5.9, a statistically significant relationship exists between per-capita GDP and education. Nations with higher per-capita GDP are associated with higher levels of education.[15]

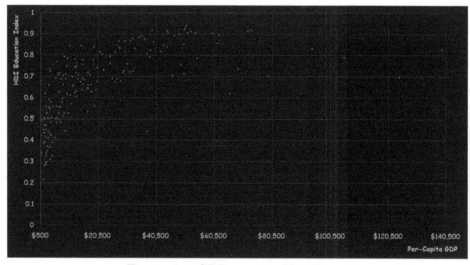

Figure 5.9: GDP versus education

■ **Health care**

Clearly, all the education in the world benefits labor little, if the health of

---

[14]Jerome Powell, "Fed Chair Jerome Powell's Address to the House Financial Services Committee," *Fed Chair Jerome Powell's Address to the House Financial Services Committee* (July 10, 2019).

[15]The *Education Index* is measured by the United Nations Development Programme for their Human Development Index (HDI). For more on this, see http://hdr.undp.org/.

the labor force is in question. Labor's health impacts efficiency, both directly and indirectly.

When school-age, individuals who are unhealthy tend to miss more classes, leading to difficulty in learning, which will negatively impact their future earning potential. Once in the labor force, decreases in a laborer's health increases the level of absenteeism, limiting the productivity of labor. Government spending on pharmaceutical development and incentivizing medical education has positive externalities that increase social benefit. A nation with a longer life expectancy should experience higher per-capita GDP. As we see in figure 5.10, nations with higher levels of life expectancy are associated with higher levels of per-capita GDP.

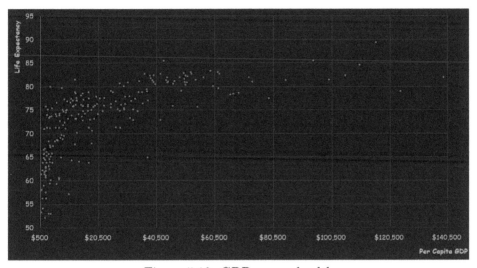

Figure 5.10: GDP versus health

5.4.3   Free Trade and Beyond

There is a preponderance of research linking the effects of various factors, like openness,[16] on growth.

For more on this, see: Xavier Sala-i-Martin's, 'I Just Ran 4 Million Regressions.'[17]

---

[16]For example, Henry Schwalbenberg and Thomas Hatcher, "Trade, Industrialization, and Economic Growth in the Philippines," *Philippine Studies* 39, no. 3 (Third Quarter 1991): 374–379.
[17]*American Economic Review* 87, no. 2 (May 1997): 178-183.

Food for Thought

1. Starting with the Solow's law of motion of capital, show how the steady state level of capital stock per unit of labor is calculated.

2. For an economy where $y = k_t^{0.3}$ and with $\delta = 0.1$, $s = 0.2$, and $n = 0.02$, calculate y^* & c^*.

3. With regard to the labor-augmenting Cobb–Douglas production function, calculate the rate at which a nation approaches its steady state.

4. Name 3 variables that, according to Sala-i-martin, are *strongly related to growth*.

   ■ What effect do they have?

Chapter 6

Money and Prices

> Money frees you from doing things
> you dislike. Since I dislike doing
> nearly everything, money is handy.
>
> Groucho Marx

The study of money (and banking) is extensive. To assume that one can do *justice* to the entirety of monetary economics in one chapter, is as foolish as it is futile. All we seek to do in this chapter is give an introduction to the topic, with enough background that further study will be that much easier.

6.1 Money and Supply of Money

There are certain misconceptions about money that many people seem to have. We begin this chapter by seeking a common definition of what we are talking about when we talk about money.

6.1.1 Functions of Money

Money, as defined by the *Oxford English Dictionary*, comes from the Anglo-Norman word *monai*, and means "Any generally accepted medium of exchange which enables a society to trade goods without the need for barter; any objects or tokens regarded as a store of value and used as a medium of exchange."[1]

Money is accepted as serving three functions:

1. Medium of exchange
   When we talk about a *medium of exchange* we mean that money can be used to purchase goods and services. In the absence of a medium of exchange, purchases are done through *barter*, which has difficulty satisfying the *double coincidence of wants,* which requires both parties in a transaction to have something that the other will take in exchange for the good.

   A now famous example of this is Kyle MacDonald's *one red paperclip*.[2] In 2005, Canadian blogger Kyle MacDonald traded a found paperclip for a fish-shaped pen, which began a year-long series of bartering, which ended in him trading for a two-story farmhouse. He claims that no trade ever included money, meaning that the house cost him a paperclip. However, he could have purchased the house earlier, if he had something that the house's original owner wanted. Money solves this problem.

2. Store of value
   When we say that money is a *store of value*, we are speaking of its ability to retain its purchasing power over extended periods of time. I can use $10 to purchase $10 worth of goods today or save it and purchase $10 worth of goods, in the future.

3. Unit of account
   The prices of goods and services are denominated in terms of how much money must be exchanged for their purchase. In this way, money is the common denomination of prices. This allows people to not only know how

---

[1]"money, n.". OED Online. March 2019. Oxford University Press. https://www.oed.com/view/Entry/880?redirectedFrom=money

[2]Ryan1Y, *One Red Paperclip* ABC 20/20, video file, 8:22, July 14, 2006, https://www.youtube.com/watch?v=BE8b02EdZvw

much things cost, but also to compare the value of different goods.

A 2019 BMW X5 SUV retails for approximately $76,000, which would buy 59.45 troy ounces of gold[3] or 2,375,149 purple m&m's.[4]

6.1.2 Measuring Money

In order to discuss money, we must differentiate between the three measures of money.

1. Currency
   Currency is the most basic form of money, consisting of notes and coins. *Paper money* is currency that counts as *fiat* money, since it has no value beyond that which is assigned to it. If the currency is made of gold, silver, or some other precious metal, it is *commodity* money, since it has intrinsic value *other* than that assigned to it, by the banks. Currency is considered the most liquid of all forms of money. The *liquidity* of money stems from how easily it can circulate, so we measure an asset's liquidity by how easily it can be transferred into currency, without losing it value.

2. M1
   M1 is a measure of money that includes currency as well as all checkable deposits. M1 includes *demand deposits, traveler's checks* and other checkable deposits. Demand deposits are what most people simply describe as checking accounts and play an important role in the *creation* of money, as we discuss in a later section.

3. M2
   M2 is a measure of money that includes everything in M1, as well as deposits in *savings accounts, time deposits*, and money market mutual funds. Savings deposits are deposits held at financial institutions that earn interest. Demand deposits are not as liquid as demand deposits. (Generally, one can purchase goods with currency or a demand deposit, not a savings account.) Time deposits, also known as certificates of deposit (CDs), are interest-bearing deposits held at financial institutions for a specific fixed term. It is expected that an individual is not going to withdraw the money from the bank until the CD matures.

Table 6.1: US supply of money, in billions

Year	Currency	M1	M2
2018	$1,628	$3,742	$14,449

---

[3]At January 1, 2019 prices
[4]m&m's, https://www.mms.com/en-us/purple-mms-bulk-candy/p/purple-mms-bulk-candy

In table 6.1 we see the measures of money for the US in 2018. Despite the fact that currency is only \$1.6 trillion, the *supply of money* is over \$14 trillion. Let's visualize the difference in size of these three measures. Figure 6.1 illustrates not only how much larger M2 is from currency and M1, but also how much more quickly it has grown in recent years.

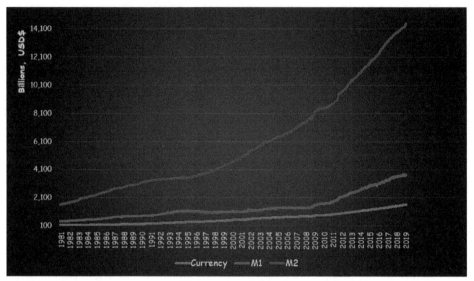

Figure 6.1: Money

6.2   Money Supply

We assume that the money supply is fixed exogenously by the monetary authority. Since 1913, *the Federal Reserve Bank* has been the central bank of the United States. The Federal Reserve is divided into three separate entities. *The Board of Governors* consists of seven governors, appointed by the president of the United States, with one member appointed as chair. The current chair is Jerome Powell. There are twelve regional Federal Reserve *district banks* across the country, pictured in figure 6.2, whose "boundaries were based on prevailing trade regions that existed in 1913 and related economic considerations, so they do not necessarily coincide with state lines."[5]

---

[5] Board of Governors of the Federal Reserve System, *The Federal Reserve System: Purposes and Functions*, 10th ed. (Washington: Board of Governors, 2016), 4.

Figure 6.2: Federal Reserve Districts[6]

The policy-making branch of the Fed is the *Federal Open Market Committee*, whose goal, along with the Board of Governors is to promote "maximum employment, stable prices, and moderate long-term interest rates."[7] In addition to conducting the nation's monetary policy, the Fed promotes the stability of the financial system, the safety of financial institutions and the payment and settlement system, and the promotion of consumer protection. The Fed's policy is made independently of Congress and the office of the president.

6.3   Money Demand

In making asset allocation decisions, investors must consider, not only, the liquidity of the asset, but also the expected return and their level of risk aversion. Money, is the most liquid of assets, has an expected return of zero, and carries no risk. The money demand decision, then, comes down to the preference of whether an individual wants to hold *money* or *non-money*. We define non-money as less-liquid assets, which, while carrying higher risk, offer a nominal return, greater than that of holding money.

---

[6]Ibid.

[7]12 USC 225a. As added by act of November 16, 1977 (91 Stat. 1387) and amended by acts of October 27, 1978 (92 Stat. 1897); Aug. 23, 1988 (102 Stat. 1375); and Dec. 27, 2000 (114 Stat. 3028).

6.3.1 Money Demand Function

The demand for money, according to Keynes, is the demand for liquidity, and therefore can be referred to as *liquidity preference*. Keynes believes that people demand money for three reasons. *Transaction* demand is based on people demanding money for the purpose of purchasing goods and services. In this way, at higher levels of income, people demand more money to increase spending. *Speculative* demand relates the relationship between money demand and changes in the nominal interest rate. At lower levels of the nominal interest rate, people have an incentive to demand money for investment purposes. The *precautionary* demand of money is based on people attempting to offset unexpected changes in income.[8]

It is generally accepted that the nominal demand for money is a liquidity function of real GDP and the nominal interest rate. The demand for *real money balances* is given by

$$\frac{M^d}{P} = L(Y_t, i_t)$$

At a given price level, given transaction demand, at higher levels of Y, the people's demand for money increases. At a given level of Y and i, if the price level increases by 4 percent, nominal demand will increase proportionally.

Given speculative demand, the demand for real money is negatively related to the interest rate. As can be seen in figure 6.3, at higher levels of i, the quantity of money demanded falls, as people prefer to hold interest-earning assets.

---

[8]According to the Board of Governors of the Federal Reserve System, "Four in 10 adults, if faced with an unexpected expense of \$400, would either not be able to cover it or would cover it by selling something or borrowing money." "Report on the Economic Well-Being of U.S. Households in 2017," Board of Governors of the Federal Reserve System (May 2018)

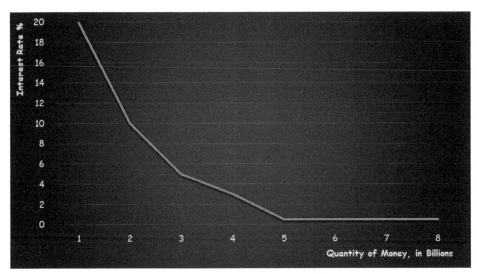

Figure 6.3: Money demand

Figure 6.4 shows the affect of increases in real GDP on the demand for real money. At higher levels of Y, the demand for money increases, reflected by a *shift* in the money demand curve to the right.

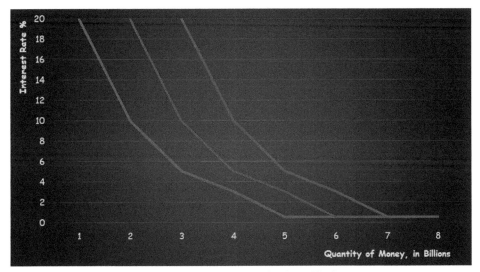

Figure 6.4: Money demand when Y changes

One notices, in figures 6.3 and 6.4, that there is a lower bound for the demand for money. The interest rate can decrease only so much before the demand for money becomes perfectly elastic. This is known as a *liquidity trap*, a topic we will discuss in a later section.

6.3.2   Putting It Together

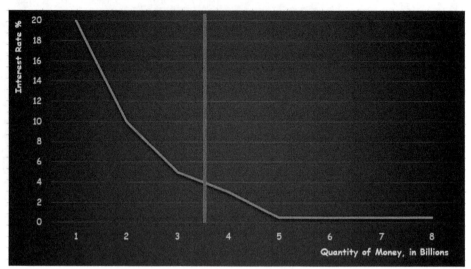

Figure 6.5: Money equilibrium

Equilibrium exists in the money market when demand for real money is equal to supply of real money, as shown in figure 6.5. We differentiate between nominal money, M, and *real* money, $\frac{\bar{M}_s}{P}$. By using $\frac{\bar{M}_s}{P}$, we are looking at changes in money, at a fixed price level. Since we assume that money supply is exogenously fixed by the Federal Reserve, whose decision is made independent of the real interest rate, the supply of real money, $\frac{\bar{M}_s}{P}$, is perfectly price inelastic.

As such, the market is in equilibrium, in figure 6.5, when the interest rate is 4 percent. If the interest rate is above 4 percent, where supply exceeds demand, there is more money than people are comfortable with at this high an interest rate. This is expected to lead to a fall in interest rates, bringing the market back into equilibrium.

As shown in figure 6.6, the changes in the supply of money affect the interest rate. As the money supply increases, we see $\frac{\bar{M}_s}{P}$ shifts to the right. In order to maintain equilibrium, interest rates fall, leading to an increase in the quantity of money demanded.

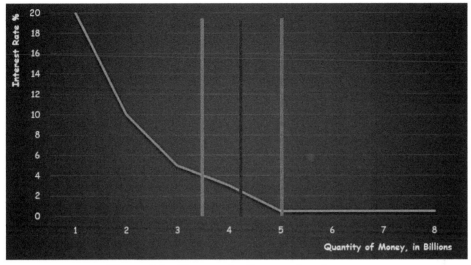

Figure 6.6: Changes in the supply of money

6.4 Money Growth and Inflation

Given the general concern over increasing price levels, one must ask how Central Bank policies affect inflation.

6.4.1 Relationship between Inflation and the Money Supply

In order to understand the consequences of increases in the money supply or, monetary expansion, let's look at the *equation of exchange:*

$$MV = PY$$

where, at a given time
   M is the supply of nominal money
   V is the velocity of money (the speed with which money circulates)
   P is the price level
   Y is real GDP

The money supply is spent a number of times in order to purchase all goods and services of a nation, at the current price level.

This can be rewritten focusing on the growth rates of the variables

$$\frac{\Delta M}{M} + \frac{\Delta V}{V} = \frac{\Delta P}{P} + \frac{\Delta Y}{Y}$$

It is often assumed that, in the absence of any *shocks* to the economy, velocity will be constant, so $\frac{\Delta V}{V} = 0$. The relationship between money *growth* and inflation, henceforth denoted by the greek letter π, therefore, can be stated:

$$\frac{\Delta P}{P} = \pi = \frac{\Delta M}{M} - \frac{\Delta Y}{Y}$$

Inflation occurs when the money supply is growing faster than real GDP. Since real GDP grows due to changes in K, L, and A, and M grows due to the exogenous decisions of the Fed, it can be said that inflation occurs when the Fed allows the money supply to grow too quickly, relative to aggregate output. Any change in the quantity of money should, therefore, lead to a proportional change in inflation.

While the growth of transactions in the economy may require *some* small amount of money growth, money growth in excess of this amount is expected to cause *inflation*. If the growth rate of real GDP is greater than the growth rate of the supply of money, the economy is expected to experience *deflation*.

6.4.2   Relationship between Inflation and Interest Rates

Now that we have a common definition of inflation, let us look at how inflation affects interest rates. Irving Fisher's 1896 book *Appreciation and Interest*[9] draws the distinction between nominal and real rates of interest.

The *nominal* interest rate is the compensation that a lender would receive for forgoing the use of his or her money, over the life of an investment. Often referred to as the *opportunity cost* of holding money, the nominal interest rate is the money you would earn if you put your money in an interest-bearing account or purchased government securities. (You can hold money for a year, and earn a return of 0 percent, or hold a bond, and earn 2.33 percent.)

The *real* interest rate, in addition to being *corrected* for inflation, is a measure of the change in the purchasing power of the money over time. If you deposit money in an interest-bearing account or purchase government bonds, you expect that your money will earn a *real* return of r. If you hold your money in currency, it is expected to earn a negative return, due to inflation. The loss of the value of your money is measured as a loss in the *purchasing power* of your money. When we say that money loses purchasing power, we are commenting on money's loss of effectiveness as a medium of exchange. (A basket of goods that cost \$100 at time t, will cost \$110 at time $t + 1$, due to inflation. You will require more money, in the future, to purchase the same basket of goods.)

---

[9]Irving Fisher, *Appreciation and Interest* (New York: Published for the American Economic Association by Macmillan, 1908).

Fisher finds that the real rate of interest can be calculated by simply subtracting inflation from the nominal interest rate. This is known as the *Fisher equation*:

$$r_t = i_t - \pi_t$$

This equation is called the *ex-post real interest rate* because it is based on the *actual* rate of inflation that occurs in a given period of time. Since neither the borrower nor the lender know, with certainty, what inflation will be in the future, borrowing/lending decisions are made based on the current *expectation* of what the inflation rate will be in the future. The real interest rate calculated by adjusting for *expected* inflation is known as the *ex-ante real interest rate*:

$$r_t = i_t - E_{t-1}\pi_t$$

The interest rate that is realized once inflation has occurred and both the borrower and lender know what it is, is the ex-post real interest rate; however, since there is no way for people to be certain about future inflation, all borrowing and lending decisions are made based on the ex-ante interest rate. As such, depending on whether actual inflation ends up being above or below the expected level of inflation, the nominal value of money borrowed/lent changes, meaning that the value of the money, at the time of repayment, will be different from the value of the money at the time it was borrowed.

Table 6.2: Effect of unexpected inflation on the interest rate

State of π	Value	Advantage
$\pi_t < E_{t-1}\pi_t$	$(i_t - E_{t-1}\pi_t) < (i_t - \pi_t)$	Lender
$\pi_t > E_{t-1}\pi_t$	$(i_t - E_{t-1}\pi_t) > (i_t - \pi_t)$	Borrower

Beautiful story:
I ask to borrow $100 from you for one year. In order for you to be willing to loan me the money, you must believe that you will receive *at least* what you would have gotten, had you put the money into an interest-bearing account or government bond. If we agree to a nominal interest rate based on an expectation of inflation that is too high ($E\pi > \pi$), you make more money on the loan than if you had bought a bond. If the expectation of inflation is too low, I end up paying you *less* than you would have received had you put your money in the bank. In this way, inflation arbitrarily shifts purchasing power from borrowers to lenders and vice versa.

6.4.3 So . . . Inflation Is Bad, Right?

We will, for the time being, assume that people are able to *anticipate* increases in price levels. As we will see in chapter 10, *unanticipated* inflation causes a whole host of additional concerns. Often, macroeconomists can be heard observing that there are only two possible problems in an economy, unemployment and inflation. While this tends to be true, it requires a clarification. As we observed in chapter 3, the real wage and real rental rates are based on the marginal products of labor and capital, respectively. *Real* variables are unaffected by changes in prices. This is called the *classical dichotomy*. Changes in the quantity of money only affect nominal variables and in the long run have no significant affect on anything real.

So, if money is *neutral*, why so much fuss over inflation?

On a microeconomic level, consumers and firms use prices to signal preferences. What quantity of a good are consumers willing to buy at a specific price? What quantity are firms willing to produce? Economists use prices to measure how markets are functioning. If we see persistent surpluses or shortages in a market, we know that prices are *too high* or *too low*, and we can predict price movements, and changes to consumer and production choices. If prices are distorted (preventing the market from clearing), it undermines their effectiveness as a signal, which is inconvenient to analysts.

Everyone has gotten a papercut in their lifetime. Papercuts are more annoying than life threatening, making people uncomfortable, depending on where they are. Inflation is like a papercut, making common activities uncomfortable.

We have already mentioned the inconvenience that inflation causes to borrowers and lenders, with regard to the random transfer of purchasing power; however, it does not stop there. The inconvenience inflation causes to households is known as the *shoe leather cost*. This is a reference to the fact that fancy shoes have leather soles. (*Really* fancy shoes have **red** leather soles.) When inflation occurs, people demand less money, not wanting to forgo the return money will earn in an interest-bearing account/investment. Given this reduced desire to hold money, people will have to make multiple trips to the bank to withdraw small sums of money to transact business, wearing down the leather on the bottom of their shoes.

When the cost of production increases, firms have to inform consumers of the change in prices. Sometimes that means increased advertising cost; in the case of restaurants, it means having to print new menus. The inconvenience inflation causes to firms is known as the *menu cost*. You may notice that some restaurants have seasonal menus or that retailers have seasonal catalogs. This allows firms to change prices every few months, to adjust to expected changes in production costs. Since different firms print menus/catalogs at different times, the differences in advertised prices may lead to confusion/distortion among consumers. (i.e., consumers may see increased price as a signal to shop/eat elsewhere).

Recently I saw *Avengers: Endgame* at my local movie theater. The movie is not only the highest grossing film of 2019 (having made over $350 million in its opening weekend, domestically), but also the highest grossing film worldwide, **of all-time**. The movie is three hours long and the ticket cost $16. The highest grossing film of 1939, *Gone with the Wind* (which made approximately $56 million domestically) was almost four hours long and a ticket cost 23 cents.

Due to inflation, it is not possible to compare the nominal box office performance of these two films, ($350 million in 2019 versus $56 million in 1939) given one was released in a year when a ticket was $0.23. If we adjust for inflation, $56 million in 1939 is equal to more than $1 billion in 2019. Clearly, analysis is complicated by changing prices, but, what of economic planning?

As hard as this may be to believe, everyone of you will, one day, get a job. As soon as you are hired, you should start saving, for your retirement. The problem is, you are not likely to retire for approximately 40 years. How are you supposed to know how much money you are going to need in 40 years, today? Assuming you decide on a quantity of savings, how much will you have to save today to ensure that you have that much saved upon retirement? As we discussed in chapter 4, intertemporal consumption decisions are based not only on income, but also on the real interest rate. If inflation is inevitable, how much inflation do you adjust for when calculating lifetime income?

Inflation is annoying, making analysis and planning difficult, but is it *never* deadly?

6.4.4   Hyperinflation

In very rare cases, price levels can increase so rapidly, that money's purchasing power erodes to a level that it *ceases* to function as a store of value, a unit of account, and in *many* cases is abandoned as a medium of exchange. *Hyperinflation*, which was formalized as a phenomena by Columbia University Professor Phillip Cagan in 1956,[10] occurs when the monthly inflation rate reaches 50 percent. When this occurs, multiple problems arise.

In a hyper-inflationary economy, people require more and more money to pursue their normal consumption. As the nation's money supply becomes less effective as a medium of exchange, people become unwilling to hold money. People begin to search for a more stable currency to use for consumption spending. With the

---

[10]Phillip Cagan, "The Monetary Dynamics of Hyperinflation," in *Studies in the Quantity Theory of Money*, ed. Milton Friedman (Chicago: University of Chicago, 1956), 25–117

increased uncertainty associated with even *moderate* inflation, money losing its ability to *store value* incentivizes people to invest their savings in some, seemingly, more stable commodity. The shoe leather costs become so high that people may abandon banking. This makes normal monetary planning impossible. With no incentive to place money in banks, the nation's banking system risks collapse. Firms, facing ever-changing prices, have the unenviable job of *constantly* reporting changes in prices, to their consumers. In Zimbabwe, in 2008, during their hyper-inflationary period, the *Los Angeles Times* reports, "At 5 p.m., July 4, a beer at a bar in Harare cost 100 billion Zimbabwean dollars . . . an hour later the price had gone up to 150 billion in the same bar."[11]

The *cause* of, (and therefore cure for,) hyperinflation is simple. Given the definition of inflation as money growth in excess of growth of real GDP, hyperinflation occurs when the quantity of money is growing too rapidly. Nations, as we discussed in chapter 4, often choose to spend more on programs than they are able to raise in taxes. In certain cases, nations finance deficit spending through the creation of money. If the nation wants to offer all citizens free education, which, let us assume, will cost $47 billion, the government could raise taxes to finance the program. The government could also *not* raise people's taxes and instead finance the $47 billion spending increase, by printing $47 billion.

$$\pi_t = \frac{\Delta M}{M} - \frac{\Delta Y}{Y}$$

Since the quantity of money is growing suddenly, rapidly, with no similar increase in real GDP, sudden, rapid inflation ensues. The revenue that the government makes by printing money is called *seignorage*. The issue with seignorage is that while the government can now finance its project, those holding money suddenly finds that the money they are holding is worth *less* than before. For this reason, seignorage is often referred to as an *inflation tax*, because it functions as a tax on anyone choosing to hold money, in the current economy.

Solution: Monetary and fiscal restraint. If the central bank slows down the growth of money, inflation will fall.

6.5   Is Deflation Better?

NO!

Think about it:
- Prices fall

---

[11]"A Crisis It Can't Paper Over," *Los Angeles Times*, July 14, 2008, https://www.latimes.com/archives/la-xpm-2008-jul-14-fg-money14-story.html.

- Firm's profits fall
- Firms cut costs (reduce L_d)
- Less labor = less income and less output
- Incomes fall
- Consumption falls
- Firm's profits fall
- Repeat

This is known as the *deflationary spiral*. As bad as inflation can be, deflation is associated with severe economic depression. Where the government and central bank may use contractionary fiscal and monetary policy to fight inflation, it is *just* as important to stimulate an economy to prevent deflation.

If unexpected inflation makes borrowers better off, since they *expect* to pay a certain real rate and when inflation is higher and the nominal rate is fixed, the real rate they pay is lower; if the economy experiences unexpected *deflation*, the opposite happens.

6.6   Principles of Money *Creation*

We have previously discussed how changes in the money supply can affect price levels. What we now must do is discuss how these changes in money growth occur. We begin by discussing the basic concept of how money is created, and what role the banking system plays.

When people discuss money *creation*, we often think of the *printing* of money. In the United States, the *Bureau of Engraving and Printing* is responsible for the printing of US fiat paper currency, while the *US Mint* is responsible for the manufacture of all US coins. As previously discussed, currency, which includes all paper money and coins, accounts for the smallest portion of what is defined as money. In order to understand how M1 and M2 are *created*, we have to discuss the structure of the banking system.

This is, by no means, a textbook on money and banking, nor is it a textbook on financial economics; however, if it *were*, I would like to title it *Finance Is Magic*. The reason this is appropriate, in part, stems from the creation of money seemingly out of nowhere, as if conjured from thin air. To understand the *magic* of money creation, we first imagine a world without magic.

6.6.1   Money Supply Under 100 Percent Reserve Banking

When one deposits money into a bank, one may imagine that his or her deposit is placed in a giant safe, kept secure until such a time as one wishes to withdraw it. This is not the case. In reality, banks are only required to hold a *fraction* of the money deposited in the bank, in reserve. Theoretically, the *reserve requirement* could be 100 percent.

If the Federal Reserve sets the reserve requirement at 100 percent, the maximum quantity of money, in the country would be equal to the quantity of currency. We would rewrite table 6.1:

Table 6.3: US supply of money under 100 percent reserves, in billions

Year	Currency	M1	M2
2018	$1,628	$1,628	$1,628

As table 6.3 shows, regardless of whether the money is held by consumers as currency or deposited into a bank as a demand deposit or savings account, no money is created beyond the money that physically exists and **currency = M1 = M2**. Under a 100 percent reserve system, since control of the the money supply is entirely in the hands of the central bank, it is believed that not only are banks more stable, but also price stability is guaranteed. While this *may* be true, 100 percent reserves creates a problems of risk and sustainability.

If banks are permitted to loan-out some fraction of the money deposited, it allows the bank to earn interest. This interest can be distributed to the people who have deposited money in the bank. This will incentivize bank deposits. In the absence of loans, the bank earns no interest, thereby removing the incentive that depositors may have. This may lead to people choosing to place their money elsewhere, in the hope of higher returns. The choice to deposit one's money with a non-regulated financial intermediary, may (and almost certainly *will*) lead to the loss of one's money. Regardless, with fewer deposits in the bank, the banking system serves little importance, being no different than placing one's money in a safe, at home. Additionally, on a microeconomic level, if the bank is not earning interest, how does the bank afford to pay its employees? How does the bank afford to offer services to its customers? Under a 100 percent reserve system, banks are non-sustainable.

No nation on Earth currently has a 100 percent reserve banking system, much to the chagrin of the *Austrian School of Economics*, whose followers, including

Ludwig von Mises,[12] Murray Rothbard,[13] and Jesús Huerta de Soto,[14] all write of its merits and the evils of *fractional-reserve* banking.

6.6.2 Money Supply under Fractional-Reserve Banking

Under a fractional-reserve system, a bank holds a portion of its deposits in reserve, allowing the balance to be loaned-out, creating liquidity for the borrowers and earning interest for the depositors. When a bank holds money in *reserve*, the money can be held physically in the bank or can be deposited in an account at the Federal Reserve.

Table 6.4: Fractional-reserve bank money creation

Deposit	Reserve	Loan	Total M
$100.00	$10.00	$90.00	$190.00
90.00	9.00	81.00	271.00
81.00	8.10	72.90	343.90
72.90	7.29	65.61	409.51
—	—	—	—
12.16	1.22	10.94	901.52
—	—	—	—
—	—	—	$1,000

The money *not* held in reserve can be used by the bank to increase the wealth of the bank. Assume a bank has a reserve requirement of 10 percent, if Bill deposits $100, the bank can loan out $90 to Sam. If Sam deposits the loaned money into the bank, the bank is able to loan out $81 of Sam's deposit to Pip. If Pip deposits the borrowed $81 into the bank, $72.90 of it can be loaned out to Mary. Each loan that the bank makes creates money equal to the value of the loan. If this behavior continues and no one withdraws the money, as we see in table 6.4, eventually, $1,000 will be deposited in the bank. The bank has *created* $900 that did not exist to begin with.

The larger the reserve requirement, the less money the bank can loan out. In the previous example, the requirement was 10 percent. Figure 6.7 shows the effect of different reserve requirements on money creation. The smaller the fraction of deposits held in reserve, the more money the bank *creates*.

---

[12]Ludwig von Mises, *The Theory of Money and Credit* (Indianapolis: Liberty Press, 1980).

[13]Murray Rothbard, *The Mystery of Banking* (New York: Richardson & Synder, 1983).

[14]Jesús Huerta de Soto, "A Critical Analysis of Central Banks and Fractional-Reserve Free Banking from the Austrian Perspective," *Review of Austrian Economics* 8, no. 2 (1995): 25--38.

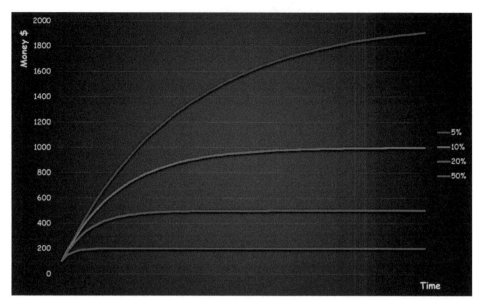

Figure 6.7: Money creation under fractional-reserve banking

To calculate how much money the banking system can create, we use the *money multiplier*. Assuming, as we did the in previous example, that consumers choose to deposit all money into the bank, the money multiplier, m, is equal to the inverse of the reserve requirement, rr.

$$m = \frac{1}{rr}$$

Table 6.5: The money multiplier

rr	m
1%	100
2%	50
4%	25
5%	20
10%	10
20%	5
50%	2

As seen in table 6.5, if a nation has a reserve requirement of 4 percent, for every additional \$1 that the central bank introduces to the economy, the banking system *creates* an additional \$25.

Bear in mind that despite the fact that the smaller the reserve requirement, the larger the multiplier effect, the more of the depositor's money the bank loans out, the more exposure the bank has to withdrawal risk. In reality, the money multiplier is affected by not only the amount of deposits that banks are *required* to hold, but also the amount that banks *choose* to hold, as well as the quantity of money that consumers *choose* to deposit.

6.6.3 Excess Reserves and the Currency Drain

The reserve requirement is a minimum that banks must hold in reserve. Banks can choose to hold *excess reserves* if they wish to guard against the risk that depositors may suddenly withdraw their money (e.g., a bank faced with a 4 percent reserve requirement can choose to hold *more than* 4 percent in reserve, to hedge against withdrawal risk). For this reason, we must consider the *desired reserve ratio*, dr, of the bank, which includes both required and excess reserves.

People are unlikely to deposit all of their money into the bank. Currency is necessary for day-to-day economic activity; as such, banks are concerned with *currency drain*, or money held outside banks, making it unavailable for money creation. Since people require currency for economic purposes, we must consider the proportion of one's currency that is deposited. The *currency-drain ratio*, cr, is the ratio of currency held *outside* banks to currency *deposited* in banks.

Bearing this in mind, the money multiplier can be rewritten:

$$m = \frac{1 + cr}{cr + dr}$$

Assuming the banks choose to hold the minimum 4 percent reserve and consumers choose to hold 20 percent in currency,

$$m = \frac{1 + 0.20}{0.20 + 0.04} = 5$$

In this case, the money multiplier would be equal to 5, meaning that for every additional \$1 that the central bank introduces to the economy, the banking system is able to create an additional \$5. If banks choose to hold an additional 8 percent in excess reserves, raising the desired reserve to 12 percent, we get a multiplier of 3.75:

$$m = \frac{1 + 0.20}{0.20 + 0.10} = 3.75$$

Excess reserves and currency drain dampen the money multiplier, eroding the banking system's influence over the money creation. This makes monetary policy more difficult, as the central bank has less ability to predict the effect of an increase of currency on the overall money supply. The smaller excess reserves and currency drain, the more *effective* monetary policy becomes.

6.7   Monetary Policy

Having seen the power of a Central Bank, let us look at how and to what end the Federal Reserve wields this power.

6.7.1   Goals of the Fed

The Federal Reserve, as the central bank of the United States, is responsible for conducting all US monetary policy with the goals set forth, as stated in 12 USC § 225a:

> The Board of Governors of the Federal Reserve System and the Federal Open Market Committee shall maintain long run growth of the monetary and credit aggregates commensurate with the economy's long run potential to increase production, so as to promote effectively the goals of **maximum employment, stable prices, and moderate long-term interest rates**.

The achievements of stable prices and maximum employment are the two key goals of the Fed, often referred to as the *dual mandate* of the Fed. Sometimes, these goals conflict, since certain policies to increase employment may be inflationary and certain de-inflationary policies may place upward pressure on unemployment. The question of how the Fed balances price stability and maximum employment when they conflict is a question of whether the Fed is made up of *hawks* or *doves*.

Hawks are Fed members who put more weight on fighting inflation to achieve the target rate. Doves are more concerned with achieving and maintaining full employment.

In order to achieve its goals, the Fed utilizes three key tools with regard to effecting changes to the *monetary base*. The monetary base of a nation is equal to the sum of all currency in circulation and reserves held by banks.

6.7.2   Tools of the Fed

■ **Open market operations**
In order to affect the quantity of money, the Fed can go into the open market and purchase or sell government securities.

If the Fed wishes to increase the money supply, it could purchase US government bonds in exchange for money. The purchase of bonds *increases* the monetary base, and the money supply will increase based on the money multiplier.

If the Fed wished to decrease the supply of money, it could sell US government bonds in the open market. The sale of bonds, in exchange for
money, reduces the monetary base, and, therefore, the supply of money.

■ **Reserve requirements**
We have already seen the effect changes to required reserves have on the
money supply. If the Fed wants to increase the money supply, it can decrease the reserve requirement, which will increase the money multiplier,
increasing the speed with which money is created.

If the Fed wishes to decrease the money supply, increases in the reserve
requirement decreases the money multiplier, slowing down the creation of
money.

■ **Discount rate**
If banks decide to hold reserves in excess of the reserve requirement, they
may choose to lend their excess to *other* banks, in need of reserves. The
interest rate that banks charge one another to borrow money is called the
federal funds rate.

At lower levels of the federal funds rate, banks have an incentive to borrow more from each other, increasing their reserves, which increases the
monetary base. The Fed targets a federal funds rate and then uses open
market operations to achieve and maintain it.

Since the Fed is the *lender of last resort*, if banks cannot raise money to
meet reserve requirements, and are unable to borrow from other banks, the
Fed extends short-term loans to banks at the *discount rate*. Increasing the
discount rate makes borrowing from the Fed more expensive. If the Fed
wishes to discourage banks from borrowing, it can raise the discount rate.

Expansionary monetary policy, or loose money, entails increases in the supply of
money. Contractionary monetray policy, or tight money, entails the shrinking of
the money supply. If the Fed wished to take part in expansionary policy, it could
buy government bonds, lower the reserve requirement, or lower the discount rate,
whereas contractionary monetary policy would entail the opposite behavior.

6.8   Additional Topics in Monetary Policy

As earlier stated, this is *not* a money and banking textbook, so there is only so
far down this particular rabbit hole we can go. That being said, there are certain
topics that are of interest to even the most basic monetary economist.

6.8.1   Conduct of Monetary Policy

According to the Fed,[15] there are three principles that make for *good* monetary policy. First, monetary policy should be consistent and easily understood by the public. If the economy is inflationary, the public should be aware of what policy the Fed will take and understand how it will work. Second, the Fed should use all applicable means to stimulate a sluggish economy and cool off an overheating one. Lastly, in order to maintain stable prices, the Fed must respond to persistent inflation with a larger increase in nominal interest rates. If inflation is persistently increasing by 1 percent, the Fed must increase nominal interest rates by *more* than 1 percent.

One way, in which the Fed can be consistent in its adherence to these principles is to follow a *rule*.

6.8.2   Taylor Rule

One rule that analysts seem fond of is the *Taylor rule*. First proposed by John Taylor in his 1993 article "Discretion versus Policy Rules in Practice,"[16] the rule suggests the relationship between changes in the nominal interest rate when the economy faces cyclical unemployment and/or inflation.

$$i_t = r_t^* + \pi_t + 0.5(\pi_t - \pi_t^*) + 0.5(y_t - \bar{y}_t)$$

where
$\quad i_t$ is the nominal interest rate
$\quad r_t^*$ is the Fed's chosen real interest rate
$\quad \pi_t$ is the level of inflation
$\quad \pi_t^*$ is the Fed's target level of inflation
$\quad y_t$ is the log of real GDP
$\quad \bar{y}_t$ is the log of full-employment GDP

According to the rule, if the economy is experiencing inflation above the target rate or output is above the full-employment level, the Fed should pursue policy that will increase the nominal interest rate, to decrease inflation. Should the economy require stimulation, due to inflation being below the target rate or output being below the full-employment level, the rule recommends decreasing rates.

While the Fed does not *strictly* consult the Taylor rule, when setting interest

---

[15]Federal Reserve Board, "Monetary Policy Principles and Practice,"
https://www.federalreserve.gov/monetarypolicy/principles-for-the-conduct-of-monetary-policy.htm
[16]*Carnegie-Rochester Conference Series on Public Policy* 39 (1993): 195—214.

rates, it still serves as an adequate explanatory tool in approximating historical U.S. monetary policy decisions.

6.8.3   The Liquidity Trap

According to Keynes, sometimes, interest rates can fall so far that monetary policy becomes ineffective. In his 1936 book, *The General Theory of Employment, Interest and Money*, Keynes introduces the concept, which John Hicks named the *liquidity trap* in 1937.[17]

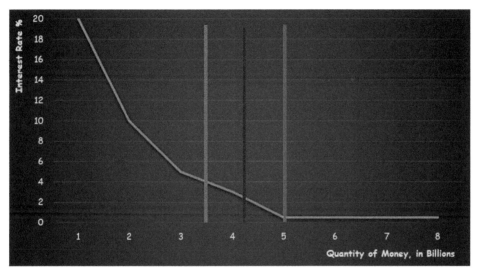

Figure 6.6: Changes in the supply of money

If we return to figure 6.6, from earlier in the Chapter, we see increases in the quantity of money lowers the interest rate; however, once the quantity of money reaches $5 billion, additional increases in the money supply fail to lower the interest rate any further. A great deal of controversy surrounds the liquidity trap, which we will discuss further, in Chapter 8.

Food for Thought

1. Using online resources, what is the current month's rate of inflation?

   ■ How does it differ from the expectation of inflation?

   ■ What is the expected rate of of inflation for next month?

---

[17]John Hicks, "Mr. Keynes and the Classics: A Suggested Interpretation," *Econometrica* 5, no. 2 (April 1937): 147–159.

2. Using online resources, what is the current nominal interest rate?

   ■ Given that, what is the current ex-ante real interest rate?

3. Using online resources, what is the current level of U.S. currency?

   ■ What is the current US M1?

   ■ What is the current US M2?

4. Read *The Economic Organisation of a P.O.W. Camp*, by R. A. Radford.[18]

   ■ How do cigarette shipments affect the price level in the POW camp?

   ■ What happens to the demand for cigarette money and the price level in the camp in the days *just* before an anticipated shipment?

---

[18] *Economica* 12, no. 48 (November 1945): 189–201.

Chapter 7

IS/LM/FE and AD/AS Model

> I'm very well acquainted, too, with
> matters mathematical,
> I understand equations, both the
> simple and quadratical,
> About binomial theorem I'm
> teeming with a lot o' news,
> With many cheerful facts about
> the square of the hypotenuse.
>
> _W. S. Gilbert and Arthur Sullivan_

Up until this point, we have built a closed economy, described its monetary system, and talked about how it grows in the long run. We must now set upon the task of describing the mechanics that rule the functioning of the economy in the short run. To do this, we will utilize the aggregate demand and aggregate supply model (**AD/AS.**)

The demand side of the economy can be described using the IS/LM/FE model, so we will begin our discussion of the model, by deriving the aggregate demand curve, using IS/LM/FE modeling, and discussing the theoretical differences between short-run and long-run aggregate supply.

$$IS: \quad \bar{Y}_t \;=\; \bar{C}(\bar{Y}_t - \bar{T}_t) + I(r_t) + \bar{G}_t$$

$$LM: \quad \frac{M}{P} \;=\; L(\bar{Y}_t,\; r_t + E_t\pi_{t+1})$$

$$FE: \quad Y^* \;=\; \bar{A}\bar{K}_t{}^\alpha L_t^{*\,1-\alpha}$$

Once we have derived the AD/AS model, we will use it in our discussion of business cycles in chapter 8.

You will recall the importance of the real interest rate in achieving equilibrium, in a closed economy, as discussed in chapter 4. In order to derive the aggregate demand curve, we must first look at all the combinations of the real interest rate, r, and real GDP, Y, at which there is, simultaneously, equilibrium in the markets for labor, goods, and money.

Equilibrium in the market for goods and services is explained in terms of the equality of savings and investment in the market for loanable funds; the market for money is explained by the equilibrium of quantity of real money balances demanded and supplied. These two relationships determine the equilibrium values of the two variables, r and Y.

7.1   Equilibrium in the Labor Market (FE curve)

The full-employment (**FE**) curve illustrates the relationship between the real rate of interest and the level of real GDP when the aggregate labor market is in equilibrium.[1] When the economy is producing with the equilibrium level of labor, L^*, (determined in the market for labor, as seen in figure 7.1), real GDP is considered at its optimal level, Y_t^*.

$$Y_t^* = \bar{A}_t \bar{K}_t^{\alpha} L_t^{*1-\alpha}$$

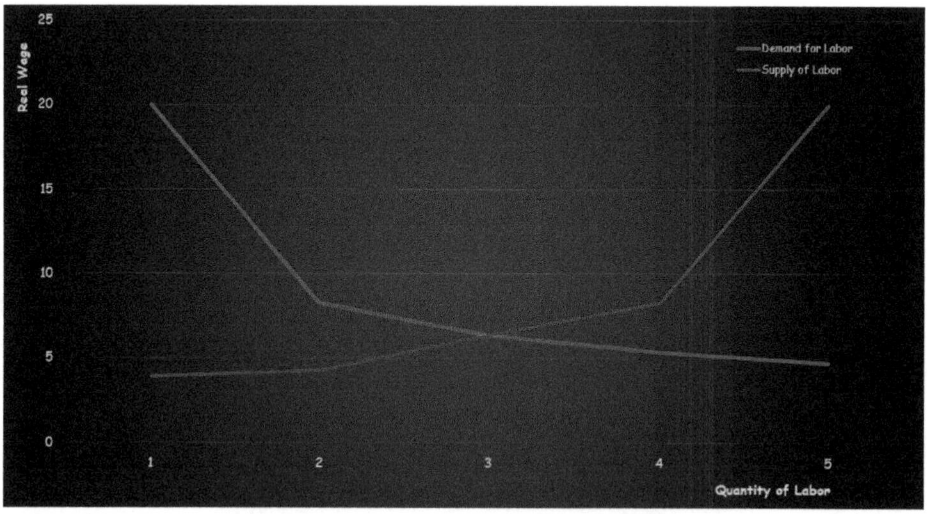

Figure 7.1: Labor market equilibrium

[1] As discussed in section 3.4.1.

When the labor market is in equilibrium, real GDP is at its full-employment level, regardless of the level of the real interest rate. For this reason, the FE curve is perfectly inelastic as seen in figure 7.2, as a vertical line at Y_t^*.

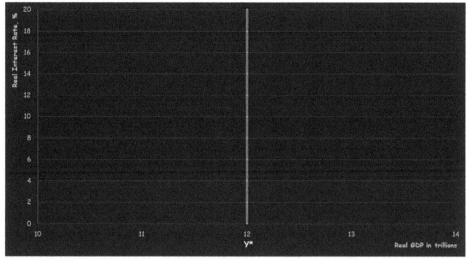

Figure 7.2: FE curve

7.1.1   Factors That Shift the FE Curve

Since full-employment is affected only by technology, capital, and labor, the only changes in Y^* are due to changes in A, K, and L, all of which cause shifts in the FE curve.

- Changes to total factor productivity (A)
- Changes to the full-employment level of labor (L^*)
- Changes to the level of capital stock (K)

7.2   Equilibrium in the Goods Market (IS Curve)

As we discussed in chapter 4, in a closed economy, the real interest rate is expected to adjust to equilibrate the market for loanable funds and the market for goods and services. For this reason, we look to the investment-savings (**IS**) curve, which reflects all of the combinations of the real interest rate and real GDP for which the market for goods and services is in equilibrium.

7.2.1 Deriving the IS Curve

Since every point on the IS curve represents a combination of r_t and Y_t for which the goods market is in equilibrium, at every point along the IS curve, the market for loanable funds is in equilibrium as well. That means that every real interest rate, at which $S_t = I_t$, corresponds to a unique level of equilibrium real GDP. As we see in figure 7.3. as real GDP changes, the real interest must adjust to maintain equilibrium in the market for loanable funds.

$$Y_t = \bar{C}(Y_t - \bar{T}_t) + I(r_t) + \bar{G}_t$$

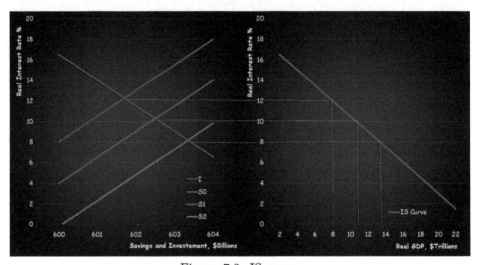

Figure 7.3: IS curve

7.2.2 Factors That Shift the IS Curve

Any shifts in savings or investment, such that the real interest rate changes, holding real GDP constant, cause a *shift* in the IS curve. These changes are known as *demand shocks*. Anything that temporarily raises spending (a *positive demand shock*), $C + I + G$, while maintaining the equilibrium level of Y, will cause the real interest rate to increase. This is reflected by a rightward shift in the IS curve. Likewise, a *negative demand shock* will cause a decrease the interest rate and the IS curve will shift left.

- ■ Consumption spending
    - Expected changes in wealth
    - Change in taxes
    - Changes in consumer confidence
- ■ Investment Spending
    - Expected changes in total factor productivity

- Changes in business confidence
- Changes in corporate taxes
■ Government Spending
- Fiscal policy

7.3 Equilibrium in the Money Market (LM Curve)

As we discussed in chapter 6, the real supply of money is exogenously set by the central bank, with no regard for the real rate of interest. For this reason, the supply of money is perfectly price elastic, with regard to the real rate of interest. The demand for real money is dependent on the liquidity function, reflecting the *negative* relationship between the demand for real money and changes in the nominal interest rate (which itself is dependent on the real interest rate and expected inflation). At higher levels of the real interest rate, holding money is discouraged, reflected by the negative slope of the money demand curve. Holding price levels and expected inflation constant, the real interest rate adjusts to equilibrate the market for money. The **LM** curve reflects all of the combinations of the real interest rate and real GDP for which the market for money is in equilibrium.

7.3.1 Deriving the LM Curve

Since every point on the LM curve represents a combination of r and Y for which the market for money is in equilibrium, every real interest rate, at which $\frac{M_s}{P} = \frac{M_d}{P}$, corresponds to a unique level of equilibrium real GDP. As we see in figure 7.4 as real GDP changes, money demand changes, requiring changes in the real interest rate to maintain equilibrium in the money market.

$$\frac{M}{P} = L(Y_t,\ r_t + E_t \pi_{t+1})$$

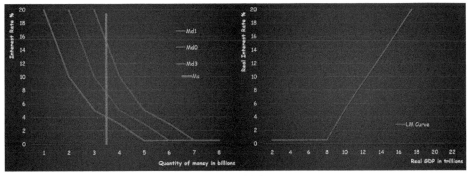

Figure 7.4: LM curve

7.3.2   Factors That Shift the LM Curve

Any factors that shift the supply or demand of real money, holding the equilibrium level of real GDP constant, cause a *shift* in the LM curve:
- Changes to nominal money supply (M)
- Changes to prices (P)
- Changes to expected inflation ($E_t\pi_{t+1}$)

7.4   General Equilibrium in IS/LM/FE Model

If one curve relates all of the combinations of r and Y for which the goods market is in equilibrium (**IS**) while the other relates combinations of r and Y for which the money market is in equilibrium (**LM**), if these are graphed on the same axis, with the **FE** model, their intersection will be the combination of r and Y for which all three markets are in equilibrium. This point of intersection is known as the *general equilibrium*, as seen in Figure 7.5.

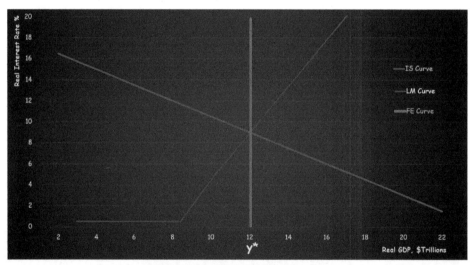

Figure 7.5: IS/LM/FE model

7.4.1   General Equilibrium in the Short versus Long-Run

As we discussed in chapter 3, in the short run prices are assumed to be sticky, and in the long run are expected to be flexible.

In the short run, disequilibrium in the market for goods (e.g., due to increased demand) will be met with firms hiring more workers to adjust to the change in the demand.

In the long run, when the market *is* in a state of general equilibrium, since we assume that the labor market is fully employed, if the goods market is in disequilibrium (e.g., demand increases), firms will adjust *prices* until the market returns to a state of general equilibrium.

7.4.2   Effects of Monetary Changes

Changes in the money supply will affect the economy differently, depending on whether prices are sticky. Assuming the economy is in general equilibrium, as seen in figure 7.5, if the central bank chooses to increase the quantity of nominal money (M), holding prices constant, $\frac{M}{P}$ will increase, causing the interest rate to fall in order to maintain equilibrium in the money market. This will cause the LM curve to shift down to the right, to LM' in figure 7.6. As a result of the decrease in the interest rate, firms increase production, seen as the equilibrium in IS/LM that falls *above* Y^*. Now, *only* the goods and money markets are in equilibrium.

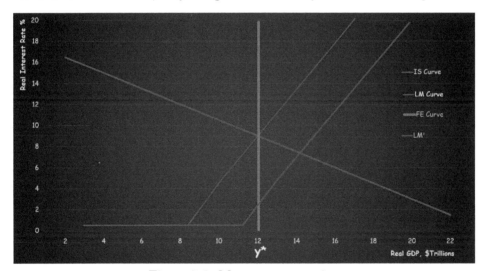

Figure 7.6: Monetary expansion

Given that the new equilibrium of IS/LM is *above* Y^*, firms respond by raising prices, while labor, noticing increases in price levels negotiates for higher nominal wages. As P increases, $\frac{M}{P}$ falls, shifting the LM curve back to its original position, in general equilibrium, however, *now* at a higher price level, due to the inflation necessary to reacquire general equilibrium. It is worth noting that, in order for the economy to return to its original general equilibrium, the increase in P must be proportional to the increase in M, just as we discussed in chapter 6.

In the long run, the monetary expansion did not affect output; all it achieved was creating inflation.

7.4.3   Classical versus Keynesian Views of IS/LM/FE Model

Although both classical and Keynesian economists believe that, in the long-run, general equilibrium will be achieved, their view of the short-run equilibrium is quite different. Macroeconomists have long argued as to just how long a time period the short run is, with *classical* economists arguing that the economy is *self-regulating*, with the automatic price adjustment mechanism bringing the market to equilibrium quickly and the *Keynesian* economists claiming that the economy will rarely operate at full employment and prices will be slow to adjust, necessitating intervention on the part of the government and the central bank.

Classical economists believe that the short-run equilibrium occurs at the point where the FE and IS curves intersect. At the real interest rate at which the labor market and goods market are in equilibrium, price levels will adjust to shift the LM curve. This works only if prices are quick to adjust to disequilibria in the money market.

Keynesian economists believe that, in the short run, the economy is in equilibrium when the IS and LM curves intersect. When there is equilibrium in the goods and money markets, it does not matter that the economy is not producing at its potential level of GDP in the short run. In the long run, the economy will be at full employment.

7.4.4   Monetary Neutrality

Given shocks to the economy, price will automatically adjust and equilibrium will be restored. Out of this belief comes the belief that *money is neutral*. Money is nothing more than a unit of measurement, so changes in prices do not have any affect on *real* variables.

In the monetary expansion example earlier, the increase in M had no effect on any of the *real* variables (Y, r, w.) All that was accomplished, by increasing the supply of money, was increases in the price level and *nominal* wages.

As mentioned, economists disagree on how fast this adjustment takes. With classical economists believing that the adjustment is immediate, they feel that money is always neutral. Keynesian economists believe that, in the short run, prices are sticky, and in the long run money is neutral; therefore, in the short run money affects the economy.

7.4.5   Effect of Changes in Productivity

Sometimes, the economy suffers temporary decreases in productivity. If productivity falls, it is reflected by a decrease in the marginal product of labor. As discussed previously, if MP_L falls, the demand for labor falls, decreasing the full-employment level of labor, L^*. This shifts the FE line to the left, as seen in figure 7.7.

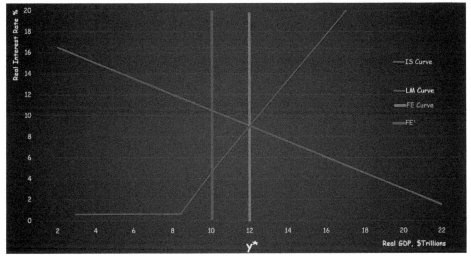

Figure 7.7: Adverse supply shock

Given that this *supply shock* is *temporary*, it causes a movement along the IS curve to a new equilibrium point between IS and FE', in figure 7.8, and has no *direct* effect on the supply or demand for money. At this new IS/FE equilibrium, with lower Y^* and higher r, price levels begin to rise, which shifts the LM curve left, giving us a general equilibrium at Y^{**}, where IS, LM', and FE' intersect.

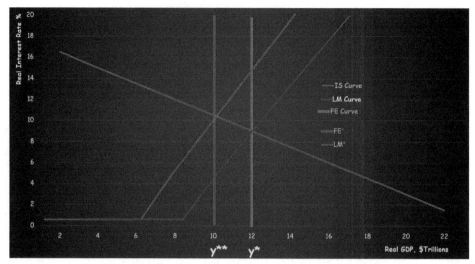

Figure 7.8: Adverse supply shock equilibrium

7.4.6 Review of Short-Run IS/LM Movements

Table 7.1: Short-Run effects of changes in IS/LM

	Δr	ΔY
Shifts to IS		
Increases in S	↓	↓
Increases in I	↑	↑
Shifts to LM		
Increases in $\frac{M_s}{P}$	↓	↑
Increases in $\frac{M_d}{P}$	↑	↓

7.5 AD-AS Model

Up to this point, we have assumed prices are constant; let us now examine what happens when price levels are allowed to change. Let us assume P falls from P_0 to P_1; holding everything *else* constant, $\frac{M_s}{P}$ increases. As the supply of real money balances increases to maintain a short-run equilibrium in the money market, interest rates need to fall. The decrease in interest rates stimulates investment spending, which leads to an increase in Y, as seen in figure 7.8, as an increase from Y^* to Y^{**}.

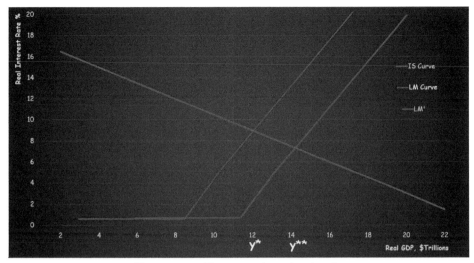

Figure 7.9: Decrease in price levels

The IS/LM curve relates to how prices affect the demand side of the economy, through their effect on interest rates. As we see in Figure 7.9, as prices decrease, $\frac{M}{P}$ increases, driving r down, leading to increases in investment spending, which increases Y.

7.5.1   Aggregate Demand (AD)

The aggregate demand curve relates how the demand side of the economy responds to changes in prices. In figure 7.9, the original equilibrium exists at the point where the IS and LM intersect. This means that given the level of nominal money, M, price level, P, expected inflation, $E\pi$, and aggregate spending, $(C+I+G)$, the markets for both money and goods and services are in equilibrium, at a level of real GDP, Y^*. When the price level falls from P_0 to P_1, we see a shift to LM', which gives us a new equilibrium with lower interest rates and higher real GDP at Y^{**}.

The AD curve directly relates the negative relationship between changes in price levels and real GDP. As we see in figure 7.10, when we move from P_0 to P_1, real GDP increases.

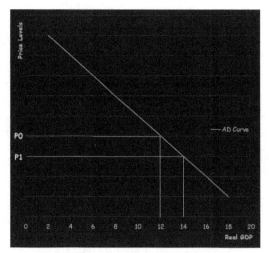

Figure 7.10: Aggregate demand

Any changes in price levels will be reflected by movements along the AD curve. Anything that shifts the IS or LM curves to the right (other than changes in P), will cause the AD curve to shift right as well.

Table 7.2: Shifts in aggregate demand

$\Delta Factor$	ΔAD
Increases in $wealth$	$\rightarrow$
Decreases in T	$\rightarrow$
Increases in expected MP_K	$\rightarrow$
Increases in G	$\rightarrow$
Increases in M	$\rightarrow$
Increases in $E\pi$	$\rightarrow$

7.5.2 Long-Run Aggregate Supply (LRAS)

Given that, in the long run prices are assumed flexible, markets are expected to clear, and as we have already discussed, output is expected to equal its full-employment level, $Y_t = Y^*$; the long-run aggregate supply curve, therefore, is equivalent to the FE curve. You will recall that the full-employment level of output is a function of the quantity of technology, A_t, capital, K_t, and labor and the full-employment level of labor, L_t^*.

$$Y_t^* = \bar{A}_t \bar{K}_t^{\alpha} L_t^{*1-\alpha}$$

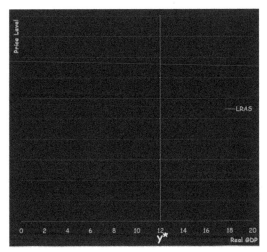

Figure 7.11: Long-run aggregate supply

Since only changes in in the production function or the market for labor affect Y^*, changes in price levels do not affect aggregate supply; in the long run,[2] the LRAS is perfectly price inelastic.

Table 7.3: Shifts in LRAS

$\Delta Factor$	$\Delta LRAS$
Increases in A	$\rightarrow$
Increases in K	$\rightarrow$
Increases in L	$\rightarrow$

---

[2]Changes in price levels do not affect wages, since when labor senses increases in P, it negotiates proportional increases in W, such that real wages remain constant.

7.5.3   Short-Run Aggregate Supply (SRAS)

■ Prices Are Fixed

The shape of the short-run aggregate supply curve is informed by whether prices are *fixed*, $\bar{P}$, in the short-run. If this is the case, firms will produce whatever quantity of output the market demands and the labor market will not be in equilibrium, since, in order to respond to a demand shock, firms will increase output without increasing prices or wages. In this case, the $SRAS$ is perfectly price elastic, as seen in the figure 7.12, on the left.

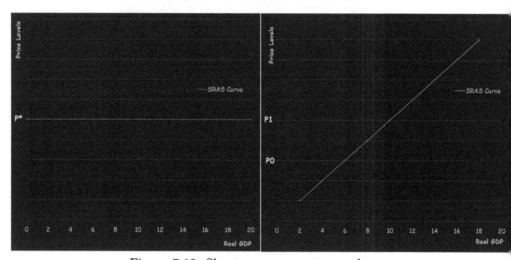

Figure 7.12: Short-run aggregate supply

■ Nominal Wages Are Fixed

If firms have the ability to change prices, when a demand shock occurs, firms will choose to raise prices, which drives the real wage down, $\frac{W}{P} \downarrow$. The lower real wage gives the firm an incentive to hire more labor, in an effort to increase output, to meet the increased demand. This movement along the firm's labor demand curve increases the quantity of labor employed above the full-employment level of labor $(L_t > L^*)$. In the short run, this increases output above the full-employment level, $(Y_t > Y^*)$, forcing unemployment to be *below* its natural rate. Since this is a change in output driven by an increase in prices, a positive relationship is seen between price levels and firms' willingness to supply goods. The SRAS has a positive slope, as seen in figure 7.12, on the right.

In the short run, since the quantity of capital, K, is assumed fixed, shifts in the $SRAS$ are seen *only* when the economy experiences changes in technology, A, or the costs of production, due to increases in the prices of productive resources *other* than labor.

Note: Nominal wages, W, are expected to adjust between the short-run and the long-run, so whether the $SRAS$ is horizontal or positively-sloped, in the short-run, the economy is expected to be at full employment, eventually.

Table 7.4: Short run vs. Long run

Short run	Long run
$L_t \neq L^*$	$L_t = L^*$
$Y_t \neq Y^*$	$Y_t = Y^*$

7.5.4 Equilibrium in the AD-AS Model

When the economy has reached its full-employment level of output Y^*, the point of equilibrium of the aggregate demand curve and both the short- and long-run aggregate supply curves is the same.[3]

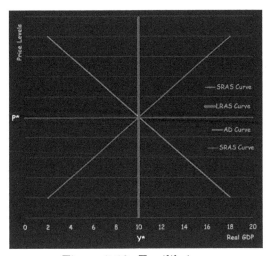

Figure 7.13: Equilibrium

Anytime the economy is in a state of disequilibrium in the short run, $(Y_t \neq Y^*)$, it is due to the labor market *not* having cleared, $(L_t \neq L^*)$. If unemployment is *below* its natural rate, $L_t > L^*$, in the short run, this means that workers are supplying more labor than they are comfortable with at the current wage. In such a case, output will *exceed* the full-employment level, as seen by the intersection of the $SRAS$ and AD curves in figure 7.14. Workers will negotiate to have an increase in nominal wages. As W increases, firm's costs of production increase, which decreases their demand for labor, clearing the labor market. When this happens, the $SRAS$ curve shifts left, bringing the economy back to its full-employment level.

---

[3]Notice that it does not matter whether you believe the $SRAS$ is perfectly price elastic.

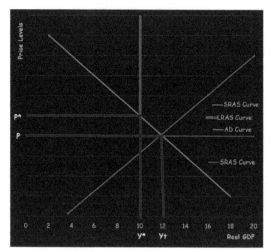

Figure 7.14: Disequilibrium

In this way, the economy is often considered, *self-correcting*; if the economy is not at the long-run equilibrium, the labor market will adjust and correct the disequilibrium.

Another way of looking at disequilibria is that firms have an expectation of what the price level should be at any given point in time. When the actual price level, P, is *above* the expected price level, EP, the economy is producing *above* Y^*. When this happens, firms adjust their expectations such that, in the long run, $EP = P$. In other words, the economy will be at its full-employment level, so long as the price level is at its expected level.

$$Y_t = Y_t^* + \beta(P - EP)$$

Using this model, we can see that the monetary *expectations* of the firm affect the short-run level of output. If price levels change *unexpectedly*, there will be a disequilibrium in the short run.

7.5.5   Expectations

There are two prevailing theories of expectations, in macroeconomics:

- Rational expectations
  People who make decisions based on the most current information available about current and future market conditions are said to have *rational expectations.*

- Adaptive expectations
  People who look at the state of the market and assume that the future will be the same as the past are said to have *adaptive expectations.*

To see the difference, let us examine inflation.

A person with rational expectations predicts future inflation, $E_t\pi_{t+1}$, having collected as much information as is available. The *actual* level of future inflation, π_{t+1}, does not differ systematically from what the person expected it to be. (The person's prediction will not consistently over- or underestimate. On average, $E\pi = \pi$.)

A person with adaptive expectations expects that future inflation will be the same as current inflation, $E_t\pi_{t+1} = \pi_t$ (i.e., if there is no inflation today, there will be no inflation, in the future).

7.5.6 Stabilization Policy

To assist the economy in the short run, to achieve and maintain general equilibrium, and to smooth out the effect of shocks, policymakers utilize *stabilization policy*. In these cases, policymakers use fiscal and monetary policy to influence movements in IS and LM (and therefore AD) to offset short-run economic fluctuations before the self-correction mechanism kicks in. The efficacy of these policies depend on one's opinions of (a) money neutrality, (b) Ricardian equivalence, and (c) crowding out.

Our discussion of expectations continues in chapter 9.

Food for Thought

1. Recall the quantity theory of money. Suppose the Fed reduces the money supply and assumes the velocity of money is constant. What happens to the AD curve?

2. According to the IS-LM model, what happens in the short run to the interest rate, income, consumption, and investment under the following circumstances?

   ■ The central bank increases the money supply

   ■ The government increases government purchases

   ■ The government increases taxes

   ■ The government increases government purchases and taxes by equal amounts

3. Assuming the nation is in a short- and long-run equilibrium, what effect would expansionary fiscal policy have, given you believe in the Ricardian equivalence?

Chapter 8

Open Market Macroeconomics

> Do you know there's other
> countries?
>
> _____
>
> Eddie Izzard, *Circle*, 2002

Since chapter 4, we have focused our discussion on a *closed* economy, with no international sector. Now that we have a basic understanding of how a closed economy functions in the short and long run, it is time to *open* the economy and see how international exposure affects the macroeconomy, by adding NX_t back into our analysis.

Once again, the aggregate expenditure model is defined as

$$Y_t = C_t + I_t + G_t + NX_t$$

8.1 Net Exports (NX_t)

As we discussed in chapter 2, *net exports*, often referred-to as the trade balance, refers to the difference between goods produced domestically for foreign consumption (exports), and goods produced abroad for domestic consumption (Imports.) If a nation's exports exceed its Imports, we say the nation has a trade *surplus*, and NX adds value to the economy. In this case, the domestic aggregate supply of goods exceeds the aggregate demand. Trade gives a vent to the surplus, adding income to the economy. If a nation's imports exceed exports, we say the nation has a trade *deficit*, and NX subtracts value of the economy due to aggregate demand exceeding aggregate supply, in which case trade fills the excess domestic demand.

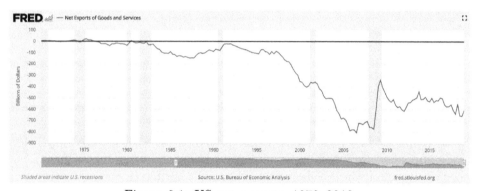

Figure 8.1: US net exports, 1970–2018

$$
\begin{array}{ll}
Y_t > (C_t + I_t + G_t) & +NX_t \\
Y_t < (C_t + I_t + G_t) & -NX_t
\end{array}
$$

If a nation is open to international trade, we say that it is an *open* economy, and we include NX; if not, we say that the economy is *closed* and omit NX. A nation can use *barriers to trade* to limit the flow of international goods or services, in the pursuit of protecting the domestic economy from foreign competition. A common measure of the level of *openness* of a nation is the quotient of the sum of a nation's exports and imports and GDP. The higher the index, the larger the impact of trade on the domestic economy.

$$Openness_t = \frac{Exports_t + Imports_t}{GDP_t}$$

Table 8.1 shows the openness index for a selection of nations for the year 2010, given data from the World Bank.[1] The reason we use 2010 is that, given that

---

[1]World Bank, "Trade (% of GDP)," https://data.worldbank.org/indicator/NE.TRD.GNFS.ZS

the World Bank has been known to make major revisions to its data for its most recent years,[2] we are more confident about data from years ago.

Table 8.1: Openness index of select countries, 2010

Nation	Openness
Brazil	22.77
United States	28.06
China	48.89
Germany	79.30
U.A.E	141.31

In table 8.1 we see that the United States, in 2010 was more open than Brazil, but less dependent on trade than the United Arab Emirates, Germany, and China.

In order to see how openness benefits a nation, let us consider a simple two-country case, in which we are the economic planners for the countries. Each country has two groups, consumers and producers, and our goal is to maximize economic welfare in both nations.

Let us consider two neighboring countries, Mullog and Noruas. Both nations operate under *autarky*. They are self-sufficient, closed economies, not taking-part in international trade.

The domestic consumers of Mullog are limited to the goods produced by Mullog's domestic producers. If Mullog opens trade with Noruas, the consumers of Mullog potentially benefit in two ways. First, with trade between the two countries, Mullog's consumers now have access to the goods of both countries. Also, since Mullog's producers are now facing international competition, this limits domestic monopoly power, keeping domestic prices lower.

On the subject of production in Mullog, prior to trade, domestic producers have access *only* to the domestic market. Opening trade with Noruas increases the market to which Mullog's producers can sell their goods. Additionally, Mullog's producers have an incentive for innovation, as a means of competing with Noruas's producers. The same is true in Noruas.

The consumers of both nations have access to a wider variety of goods at lower prices, with trade. The producers of both nations have the opportunity to sell to a larger market, which may stimulate production and therefore employment in both countries. The increased employment and spending in both countries can lead to long-term economic growth.

---

[2]Giacomo Santangelo, "International Data Revision: Theory and Analysis", *Asian Journal of Public Affairs* 1, no. 1 (2007): 7–19.

This is, of course, an oversimplification however, it is not too far from what international trade offers a nation.

8.1.1 Barriers to Trade

In order to discuss international trade in the 21st century, we must recognize the growing *anti*-globalization movement. In his book, *The Lexus and the Olive Tree*,[3] Thomas Friedman presents a picture of a global economic system bifurcated into *modern* economies (progress through openness, technology, and investment in human capital) and *traditional* economies (preservation of ancient, traditional values and nationalism). According to Friedman, the modern economies will attempt to spread to all the nations of the globe, while they experience some push-back from the traditional economies.

There are few motivations for anti-globalist behavior. Often governments will claim the need for economic protection on the grounds of fear of *loss of sovereignty* or *cultural identity* (e.g., Brexit) or shielding the domestic workforce from cheap foreign labor (e.g., the battle against *off-shoring*). While there **is** an argument to be made for protecting *infant industries* from competition for a *short* period of time, until they can become competitive, *rarely* is this the reason used. And when it *is*, it is often abused.[4]

Nations wishing to limit international economic exposure have always possessed the tools to do so. These barriers include (but are not limited to)

- Tariffs
  When a nation places a *tax* on a foreign good being imported, this is known as an *import tariff*. The tariff raises the domestic price of the import relative to the domestically produced good. Tariffs are a tool used to influence domestic consumer spending *away* from foreign-produced goods. As with any other tax, a tariff distorts the market for the good; if the distortion

---

[3]Thomas L. Friedman, *The Lexus and the Olive Tree* (London: HarperCollins, 2000).

[4]At the end of the US Civil War, the US was concerned with reconstruction and needed to protect domestic industry. To this end, the US Congress put into place a complex system of protectionist policies, which, in 1882, a commission appointed by US President Chester Arthur recommended be reduced. The result was the Tariff of 1883. Without going too deeply into the specifics of the tariff, one item of note, imported fruit, was exempt from tax. This lead importers of tomatoes to file for a tariff exemption, due to the fact that tomatoes are classified as fruit. In 1893, the US Supreme Court ruled, in *Nix v. Hedden* that, for the purposes of the tariff, a tomato is a vegetable, and therefore is not exempt from tax.

is significant, it can lead to *market failure*.[5] At the very least, the tariff reduces the economic welfare of domestic consumers, since they have less affordable consumption options, in the *hope* of increasing the welfare of domestic producers.

■ Quotas[6]
A numerical limit, placed on the quantity of a foreign good that can be imported, is an *Import Quota*. A Quota, like a tariff, limits the domestic consumer's access to the foreign-produced good. Also, like a tariff, quotas distort the market for the good, in the hope of benefiting the domestic producer, at the expense of the domestic consumer.

The success of a barrier to trade is predicated on an exporting nation **not** retaliating. In the earlier example, if Mullog places a tariff or quota on goods imported from Noruas, it will only be effective if Noruas does not place trade restrictions on goods exported from Mullog.

Regardless of the manner of trade restriction implemented by a nation, the *burden*, ultimately falls on the domestic consumer. When the burden proves too much, the government is pressured to remove the restriction. In this manner, the issue is decided.

For more detail on the trade relationship the United States has with other nations, see the United States Trade Representative's website, ustr.gov/.

8.1.2   Trade = Finance

You will recall from chapter 4 that, in a closed economy, in order to achieve equilibrium in the goods market, we expect the real interest rate to adjust in the market for loanable funds.

$$\bar{Y}_t = \quad \bar{C}_t + I_t(r_t^*) + \bar{G}_t$$
$$I_t(r_t^*) = \quad \bar{S}_t$$

The equilibrium real interest rate, r_t^*, is such that national saving equals investment demand, simultaneous to domestic product, equaling domestic expenditure. In a closed economy, it is assumed that $I_t(r_t^*) = \bar{S}_t$; however, in an open economy, no such assumption is made given that the market for loanable funds now includes an international component.

In an open economy investment does not need to equal national saving, given

---

[5]The allocation of goods in the market is inefficient, due to *imperfect Competiton, imperfect information, and incomplete markets.*

[6]An import quota set to *zero* is known as an *embargo*.

national saving $\bar{S}_t = \bar{Y}_t - \bar{C}_t - \bar{G}_t$ and investment, I_t must now account for international borrowing/saving. In a closed economy, if investment demand exceeds savings, the real interest rate rises, causing investment demand to decrease, bringing the market into equilibrium. In an open economy, if there is a shortage of loanable funds, individuals can borrow from foreign lenders with no change to the real interest rate. Likewise, if savings exceeds investment, the excess savings will be lent to borrowers abroad. In an open economy, we talk about *net capital outflow*, which is defined as the difference between national savings and investment.

Since net exports is equal to the difference between national income and domestic spending,

$$NX_t = \bar{Y}_t - (\bar{C}_t + I_t + \bar{G}_t)$$

and national savings is equal to the difference between national income and consumption and government spending

$$\bar{S}_t = \bar{Y}_t - \bar{C}_t - \bar{G}_t$$

Net exports can be rewritten:

$$NX_t = \bar{S}_t - I_t$$

In equilibrium, the flow of goods and services will equal the flow of international capital. If a nation has a trade *surplus*, it will also have excess savings, making it a lender of capital. A nation running a trade deficit has a shortage of saving, relative to its investment demand.

8.2 Exchange Rates

The discussion of international trade is really a discussion of the supply and demand of foreign goods. Supply and demand decisions always involve the consideration of prices. Regardless of what country a consumer is purchasing a good in, firms want to be paid in *their* local currency. If you wish to celebrate a joyous occasion by purchasing a bottle of champagne, you may spend $170 for a 2006 bottle of Veuve Clicquot, *La Grand Dame*, at your local liquor store; however, in order for the liquor store to *import* that bottle, the producer had to be paid in Euro. So, in demanding the import of a French good, you are *technically* demanding French currency.

8.2.1 Nominal Exchange Rates

The amount of one nation's currency it takes to purchase a unit of another nation's currency is the *nominal exchange rate, e.* Table 8.2 shows the nominal exchange rates of a selection of six currencies compared to the US dollar, on the first two days of 2019. Notice that, on January 1, the US dollar could have purchased 6.8797 units of the Chinese currency, or 3248.0672 units of the Colombian currency, in the foreign exchange market.

$$e = \frac{Foreign\ Currency}{\$}$$

Table 8.2: Select US nominal exchange rates[7]

Currency	Jan. 1, 2019	Jan. 2, 2019
Brazilian real	3.8804	3.7994
British pound	0.7848	0.8016
Chinese yuan renminbi	6.8797	6.8591
Colombian peso	3248.0672	3237.5722
Euro	0.8724	0.8819
UAE dirham	3.6722	3.6741

Since nominal exchange rate, is a relative measure, this also shows that on the first of January 2019, it would require approximately 3,248 Columbian pesos to purchase 1 US dollar in the foreign exchange market.

When a currency strengthens, or *appreciates*, relative to a foreign currency, the quantity of the foreign currency that one unit of the domestic currency can purchase has increased, $e \uparrow$. Notice that between the first and second days of 2019, the US dollar appreciated relative to the pound, the euro, and the dirham. When the US dollar appreciates relative to a foreign currency, it can also be said that the foreign currency depreciated relative to the dollar. When a currency weakens, or *depreciates* relative to another currency, the quantity of the foreign currency that can purchased has decreased, $e \downarrow$.

8.2.2   Real Exchange Rates

Knowing the quantity of one nation's currency that can be purchased with 1 US dollar does not give us any information as to what can be done with the foreign currency once it has been acquired (i.e., \$1 = 3248 Columbian pesos. Does 3,248 Columbian pesos buy \$1 worth of goods?). The *real exchange rate* is the price of domestic goods relative to the price of foreign goods and is calculated by multiplying the nominal exchange rate (e) (pesos per dollar) and a ratio of price levels of the domestic (P) and foreign countries, (P^f).

$$\rho = e \times \frac{P}{P^f}$$

With the real exchange rate we are relating the value of the goods in each country, so another way of looking at the real exchange rate is the rate at which domestic

---

[7]"Exchange Rates," https://www.exchange-rates.org/

goods can be traded for those produced in other countries. When the real exchange rate *increases*, the value of the foreign goods has fallen relative to the value of domestic goods. When this happens, we expect domestic imports to increase and exports to decrease, leading to a decrease in NX. Net exports are a function of the real exchange rate. At higher levels of ρ, domestic consumers see that domestic goods are more expensive than foreign goods, and demand more foreign goods, and imports increase. Likewise, consumers in other countries will demand fewer exports due to the higher relative price, so exports fall.

$$NX_t(\rho) = \bar{S}_t - I_t(r_t^*)$$

In an open economy, the real exchange rate will adjust to equilibriate trade as well as net capital flow.

8.2.3   Purchasing Power Parity

Theoretically, if two goods are identical, their price should be equivalent. If the goods are produced in different countries, but are identical, the only difference in their price will be that they are denominated in the respective currency. If the prices are *not* equivalent, the exchange rate will adjust to a level that will equate the price of the good between nations.

When this is true for one good, we refer to it as the *law of one price*. In cases when the identical good is *not* price equivalent, arbitrage will adjust the price in the two markets. When the nominal exchange rate has adjusted to equate the price levels of the two nations, this applies to *all* goods. In this case, the purchasing power of the two currencies is equivalent.

$$e = \frac{P^f}{P}$$
$$\rho = e \times \frac{P}{P^f} = 1$$

One of the most popular tools in the discussion of purchasing power parity is the *Big Mac Index.*[8]

Burgernomics

The *Big Mac* is a sandwich that US fast-food giant McDonald's has been manufacturing since 1967. Whether you buy it in New York City, Paris, or Moscow, the Big Mac is made the same way all over the world.[9] The *Big Mac Index* was developed by *The Economist* in 1986 and posits that since a Big Mac is produced

---

[8]"The Big Mac Index," *The Economist*, July 10, 2019, https://www.economist.com/news/2019/01/10/the-big-mac-index
[9]India offers a *Maharaja Mac*, which contains no meat.

the same way, all over the world, if a sandwich costs \$4 in the US, the price in *every* country should be the local currency equivalent of \$4. If this is not the case, it is believed that the nominal exchange rate will adjust to make it so.

This, of course, will not occur in the real world. In order for purchasing power parity to occur, goods must be identical and freely-traded. While a Big Mac in NYC may *seem* identical to one produced in Moscow,[10] the sandwich is a *non-tradable* good, making arbitrage impossible. The existence of non-tradable goods and barriers to trade make PPP impossible to achieve. While *absolute purchasing power parity*, in which exchange rates adjust to equate price levels between both countries, is impossible, exchange rates do tend, in the long run, to move in the direction suggested by the theory.

8.3   Exchange Rate Determination

Nominal exchange rates are determined in the market for foreign exchange. Anything that affects the supply and demand for the currency will influence the equilibrium exchange rate.

People demand a nation's currency for a number of reasons, generally stemming from trade or finance. If people wish to purchase a nation's exports, or purchase financial assets of a nation, they will require that nation's currency. Increases in the demand for exports or financial assets increases the demand for that nation's currency.

When consumers demand an import or wish to purchase a foreign financial asset, they supply domestic currency in exchange for the foreign currency. Increases in the demand for foreign goods or assets increases the supply of the domestic currency. Equilibrium in the market for foreign exchange occurs when the supply of the currency is equivalent to its demand. Having equilibrium in the market for foreign exchange also means that there exists balanced trade. If there is disequilibrium, the exchange rate will adjust to equate the value of imports and exports.

To better see this, let us consider the United Arab Emirates.

The US and the UAE have enjoyed free trade for quite some time now, boosted since signing the *Trade and Investment Framework Agreement*[11] in 2004. In 2018, US exports to the UAE totaled \$19.5 billion, with imports from UAE totaling

---

[10]They both are two all-beef patties, special sauce, lettuce, cheese, pickles, and onions on a sesame bun.

[11]"US-United Arab Emirates TIFA,"
https://ustr.gov/sites/default/files/uploads/agreements/tifa/asset_upload_file305_7741.pdf

approximately $5 billion. This gives the US a $14.5 billion trade surplus with the UAE.

The US import of $5 billion worth of UAE goods, requires the demand of $5 billion worth of dirham. In this way, the US demand of AED is also the US demand for UAE imports. Likewise, the UAE demand to import $19.5 billion worth of US goods requires the demand of $19.5 billion US dollars, for which the UAE exchanges dirham. In this way, the supply of dirham is the demand for US exports. If the US has a trade *surplus* with the UAE, the market for dirham will not be in equilibrium.

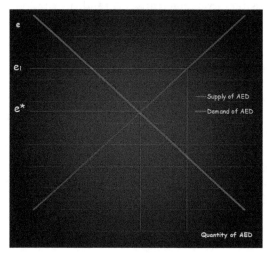

Figure 8.2: Foreign exchange market for dirham

Figure 8.2 shows the market for the UAE currency, the dirham (AED) in terms of the US dollar, with e^* being the nominal exchange rate at which the supply of dirham equals the US demand. In this example, $e = \frac{AED}{\$}$. Notice that, at e_1, the supply of dirham is greater than the demand. In this case, the market will adjust, causing a depreciation of the dirham relative to the dollar. As the dirham weakens relative to the dollar, it takes more dirham to purchase dollars, making US exports more expensive, and UAE exports cheaper, bringing the market for dirham into equilibrium at point e^*.

Table 8.3: Factors affecting US currency exchange

Demand for UAE dirham	Supply of UAE dirham
Demand for UAE exports	UAE demand for imports
Demand for UAE assets	U.A.E demand for foreign assets
Tourism in the UAE	UAE tourists abroad

Given the market's ability to adjust, trade surpluses are expected to be met with a depreciation of the currency, leading to increases in imports and decreases in exports; likewise, trade deficits are expected to be met with appreciations of the currency.

Trade Balance	Currency	NX
Surplus	Appreciation	$NX \downarrow$
Deficit	Depreciation	$NX \uparrow$

8.3.1   Changes in the Foreign Exchange Market

Since exchange rates are a relative measure, changes in the market for foreign exchange are based on relative changes.

Inflation

If US price levels are increasing faster than those in other countries, foreign consumers will find US exports less desirable, driving both US and foreign consumers away from the consumption of US goods, depreciating the currency.

Interest Rates

If US interest rates increase, relative to interest rates of other countries, foreign investors have an incentive to invest in the US, necessitating an increase in demand for the US dollar, causing an appreciation in the currency.

Growth Rates

If US GDP is growing faster relative to other countries, it is expected that the US demand for imports will be increasing faster, as well. If the demand for imports is growing, this will put pressure on the value of the US dollar, causing a depreciation, relative to other currencies.

Now, a Warning

Let us not forget that we are talking about a market, and markets, on a microeconomic level, are affected by expectation. If people *expect* a movement to occur, in a market, even if there is no good reason for it, in the short-run, the market tends to move that way. For this reason, we must always be aware that the market is subject to volatility given changes in people's expectations.

8.4   Fixed versus Flexible Exchange Rates

In a *flexible* or *floating exchange rate* system, exchange rates are determined by the demand and supply in the foreign exchange market. Under a floating system, any changes that are seen in the rate due to changes in the supply and demand for the currency. In a floating system, increases in the demand for the currency are reflected as *shifts* in the demand curve. (e.g., an increase in the demand for UAE exports will shift the dirham demand curve right, driving e up).

Under a floating exchange rate system, any trade disequilibria will automatically be cured, given movements in rates. Any demand or supply shocks will lead *only* to temporary disturbances to the international sector.

The issue that is raised by the floating system is that, given the freedom the market has to adjust to disequilibria, in trade, the market is open to volatility, which may affect consumer/investor confidence.

Under a *fixed exchange rate* system, exchange rates are set at an officially predetermined level. In order to maintain this level the central bank commits to buy and sell the nation's currency at that rate to ensure maintenance. Under such a system, economic confidence is higher, due to the belief in the stability of the currency. With less uncertainty over future movements in trade prices, firms and consumers can better plan for the future, incentivizing international investment.

8.5   IS/LM in an Open Economy

Having already covered the basic mechanics of the AS/AD model in chapter 7, for a closed economy, adding an international sector to the economy poses little difficulty.

Given that nothing has changed in the market for labor or money, the addition of the international sector affects neither the FE nor LM curves. To see how the IS curve is affected, let us look to the goods market equilibrium formula, with international trade:

$$Y_t = \bar{C}_t(Y_t - \bar{T}_t) + I_t(r_t^*) + \bar{G}_t + NX_t(\rho)$$

Any event that increases NX, at given levels of the real interest rates and real GDP, will shift the IS curve to the right. These events include, increases in foreign GDP, which it is assumed would increase foriegn demand for domestic exports; increases in the interest rate of the foriegn country, which it is assumed will incentivize foreign investors to borrow domestically; and, any change in global tastes and preferences, which lead to increases in demand for domestic exports. Bearing in mind that the the real exchange rate will adjust to equate NX with $S - I$, increases in r, relative to other nations, are expected to increase excess savings and foreign investors have an incentive to invest in the US, necessitating an increase in demand for the US dollar, causing an appreciation in the currency. This ultimately leads to a decrease in NX.

8.5.1   Stabilization Policy with Fixed Exchange Rates

Since a new component has been added to the AS/AD model, we should examine how the government and central bank's ability to smooth economic fluctuations is affected. For the purposes of this example, let us return to the nation of Mullog, last seen in chapter 5.

Open Market Fiscal Policy

Let us assume that Mullog has balanced trade and a flexible exchange rate and is currently experiencing a period of recession. If the government decides to cut taxes and/or increase government spending in the hope of stimulating the economy, what happens? Increases in G and/or decreases in T will cause a rightward-shift in AD. With the increase in AD also comes an increase in the demand for imports, casting Mullog into a trade deficit. This is known as *international crowding-out*. A portion of the benefit of expansionary fiscal policy will be offset by the increase in imports that it stimulated. In the case of a trade deficit, we expect Mullog's currency to depreciate to once again balance trade.

However, with the initial increase in aggregate demand, the demand for money also increases, since the liquidity function states that M_d is positively related to changes in Y. The increase in the demand for money increases the real interest rate, which will lead to *decreases* in real GDP. With the increase in r, it is expected that the exchange rate will appreciate, due to the increase in the foreign demand for investment in Mullog.

The efficacy of fiscal policy, in this case, is dependent upon understanding which outcome is more significant, the increase in the real GDP and price levels or the increase in the real interest rate.

Open Market Monetary Policy

If, rather than relying on Fiscal Policy, the central bank chooses to stimulate the economy by increasing the supply of money, the expansionary policy will lead to a decrease in the real interest rate, shifting AD to the right, leading to increases in both price levels and real GDP, in the short-run. The increase in real GDP and price levels, relative to the rest of the world, will lead to increases in the demand for imports (due to the increase in Mullog's real GDP) and decreases in the foreign demand for exports (due to the increase in price of Mullog's goods). Mullog now has a trade deficit.

This trade deficit will lead to a depreciation of Mullog's currency, which will increase exports and decrease imports, increasing NX and shifting AD further to the right.

Remember, in the long run, money is neutral, having no real effect on real variables; however, in the short run monetary policy is more effective than fiscal policy at stimulating a recessed economy. Since the source of crowding out is the increase in the real interest rate associated with expansionary fiscal policy, the central bank can hold the real interest rate constant and there will be no crowding-out.

Food for Thought

1. Using online resources, what is the current nominal exchange rate, between the US dollar and the Thai bhat? (dollars per bhat)

   ■ The US dollar and the Qatari rial?

   ■ The US dollar and the euro?

2. Using online resources, what is the average price of a Big Mac in the United States, Qatar, and Europe?

   ■ Based on this, what *should* happen to the nominal exchange rates?

   ■ Is it likely to happen? Why (or why not?)

3. *An empirical experience*

   ■ Look at the clothes you have on, right now. When you are safe and alone in your dorm room, examine the tags on the clothes you have on. In what countries were the clothes made?

   ■ Make a list of the nations of origin of each of the items of clothing you have on.

■ What is the currency of the nation(s) of origin?

■ What is the nominal exchange rate between the US dollar and the currency of the nation(s) of origin of your clothes?

■ Go to the website of the US trade representative. What trade relationship does the US enjoy with the nation of origin?

■ What percentage of the total amount of US imports come from that nation?

■ What percentage of that nation's exports does the US account for?

4. *An additional experience*

■ Go to the produce section of your local grocery store.

■ Pick-up a banana. In what country was it grown?

■ What is the exchange rate between the US dollar and the nation of origin of the banana?

■ Walk around the produce section and look at the nations of origin of the various fruit and vegetables. Make a list of nations of origin.

■ What is the nominal exchange rate between the US dollar and the nations of origin of the produce?

■ Go to the website of the US trade representative. What trade relationship does the US enjoy with the nation of origin?

■ What percentage of the total amount of US imports come from that nation?

■ What percentage of that nation's exports does the US account for?

Chapter 9

Business Cycles

> Normal is nothing more than a cycle on a washing machine.
>
> ———————————————
>
> Whoopi Goldberg

The periods of economic fluctuation, often referred to as the cycle of boom and bust, is known as the *business cycle*. A business cycle is the recurring period of time in which all aspects of the economy experience expansion, followed by contraction, followed by expansion, *ad infinitum*. Business cycles fluctuations are seen in all economic activity, not just production.

The classical model attributes expansion to exogenous factors, such as weather conditions or technical progress. Keynesians attribute expansion to such endogenous factors as fiscal and monetary policy, as well as government regulation.

A business cycle involves four main stages:

1. Expansion
   The expansion stage of the business cycle is marked by improvements in various economic variables.

2. Peak
   At some point, the economy will reach its highest level in the cycle, after which it will begin to contract. This turning point is its *peak*.

3. Recession
   A recession is the contraction of the economy, during which the performance of various economic indicators worsen. The most severe recession is called a *depression*.

4. Trough

At some point, the economy *bottoms out.* Once this occurs, the economy heads into recovery and the cycle begins anew. This turning point is its *trough.*[1]

9.1 *Cycles* in the Data

The timing and directionality of the cyclical behavior of economic variables during a business cycle are worth noting for two reasons. Whether a variable moves *with, against,* or is *unaffected* by aggregate economic activity allows analysts and policymakers to better adjust to the business cycle.

Pro-cyclical variables increase as the economy expands and decrease as it recesses.

Counter-cyclical variables move against the business cycle, decreasing during an expansion and increasing during a recession.

If a variable is *leading* the economy, its turning point occurs before the business cycle.

If a variable is *coincident,* its turning point occurs concurrent with the business cycle.

If a variable is *lagging* the economy, its turning point occurs after the business cycle.

Let us, for a moment, look at some variables and how they are affected by business cycles.

---

[1] As stated by the National Bureau of Economic Research (NBER).

■ Output, Welfare and Spending

As seen in figures 9.1 through 9.4, real GDP and per-capita real GDP and consumption and investment expenditure are all pro-cyclical and coincident.

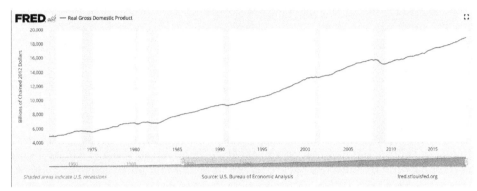

Figure 9.1 Real GDP, 1970–2018

Figure 9.2 US per-capita real GDP, 1970–2018

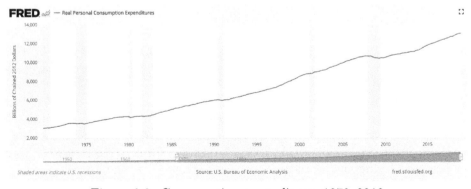

Figure 9.3: Consumption expenditure, 1970–2018

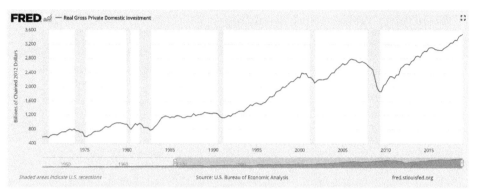

Figure 9.4: Investment expenditure, 1970–2018

Figure 9.5 shows net exports for the US from 1970 through 2018. The response of net exports to the business cycle is a bit more complicated, given that there are two forces at work. When an economy is expanding, it is expected that imports will be increasing, as well, meaning imports are expected to be pro-cyclical and coincident; however, exports are influenced by the business cycles in the rest of the world. In this way, the business cycles of one country can be amplified by the business cycle expansions of their trading partners.

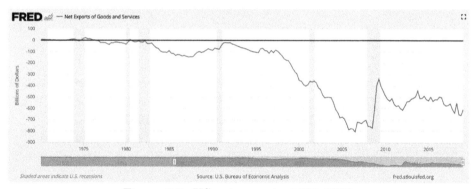

Figure 9.5: US net exports, 1970–2018

■ Unemployment

As we see in figure 9.6, unemployment is counter-cyclical and coincident. This feels intuitive, given the effect that unemployment has on production within the country. If the economy is doing *poorly*, we expect firms to either lay off workers or postpone hiring new workers.

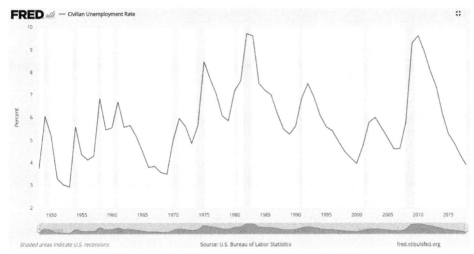

Figure 9.6: US unemployment, 1948–2018

■ Price Levels

Given the effect monetary policy has on the economy, we expect monetary growth to be pro-cyclical and lead the economy. Inflation is expected to also be pro-cyclical, given that when the economy expands, prices should increase, but only after a time. Since inflation occurs only *after* the expansion begins, it lags the economy.

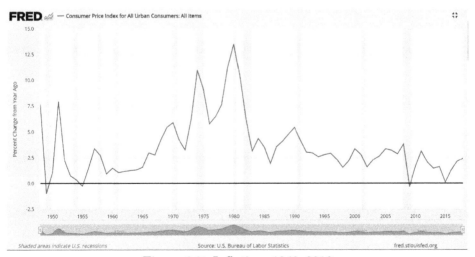

Figure 9.7: Inflation, 1948–2018

■ Stocks, Bonds & Leading Indicators

Stock prices, as seen in figure 9.8, tend to be pro-cyclical and lead the economy. An asset's current market price is the net present value of a *perceived* future stream of income (e.g., How much income[2] will I receive over my investment horizon.[3]?). That said, current equity market price is based on people's *perception* of the value of the companies. If people's perception changes, the equity prices change. When people perceive the future looks bright (due to news, for example), equity prices *rises*. When people perceive the future looks dim, the equity prices fall. When there is uncertainty (people do not have a common vision of the future), there is volatility in the market. Since the value of equity is the present value of an *expected* stream of future income, falling stock prices presage a decrease in investor confidence. For this reason, the economy going into recession is generally proceeded by the stock market turning bearish. A bull market is considered a sign that the economy is in the expansion stage of the cycle, with the creation of market *bubbles* indicating that the economy will soon reach its peak, after which recession is soon to come. Using equity markets to predict the future state of the economy has its dangers.[4]

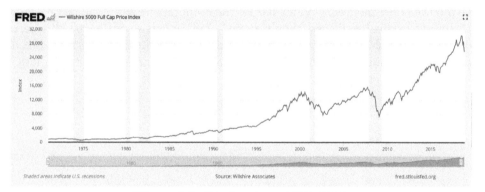

Figure 9.8: Stock prices, 1970–2018

The longer the term of a loan, the higher the interest rate a lender requires to be paid. For this reason, the difference between the interest rate paid on long-term debt contracts *should* be higher than the interest on short-term contracts.

---

[2]Dividends, interest, capital gain, etc.

[3]The time I hold the asset

[4]**Warning:** There are two groups in any market, *investors & speculators*. Investors enter the market because they have a belief that the assets they hold will appreciate in value, over time. Speculators are invested in an asset for a shorter period in the hopes of making a *quick buck*. When the market is driven by investors, and information about assets is free, the market value of an asset is accurate. When the market is driven by speculators or information is imperfect, the market is distorted (under- or overvalued). If the market is overvalued, at some point, the market *corrects* to, what investors feel is the true market value.

When the interest rate on short-term debt becomes *higher* than the interest rate of long-term debt, it is said that the yield curve has *inverted*. This occurs when investors expect inflation to remain low as well as expect the economy to contract.

The measure used by *The Conference Board*[5], when constructing their *Index of Leading Economic Indicators*, is the difference between 10-year Treasury bond rates and the federal funds rate. Figure 9.9 shows this relationship. When the line drops below zero, the short-term rates are higher and the yield curve is inverted, signaling a recession. When the line is above zero, long-term rates are higher than short-term rates, signaling inflationary growth.

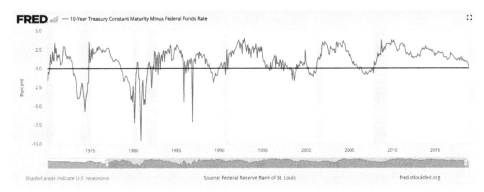

Figure 9.9: Yield spread, 1970–2018

There are many indicators that analysts and policy-makers use in order to attempt to predict future economic fluctuations. As I recently mentioned, The Conference Board calculates a *Leading Economic Index (LEI)* which, according to their website, is a composite index of "leading, coincident, and lagging indexes designed to signal peaks and troughs in the business cycle for major economies around the world." Specific attention must be paid to the *LEI*, since, it is believed that decreases in the index for more than three consecutive months signals recession.

The components[6] of the *LEI* include the previously mentioned interest rate spread, manufacturing sales, the average duration of unemployment, as well as building permits for new private housing units, seen in figure 9.10.

The decision to build a new house signals positive expectations for the future. When *Housing Starts* fall, we see it often signaling an eminent recession.

---

[5]The Conference Board, https://www.conference-board.org/us/

[6]The complete make-up of the *LEI* can be found at The Conference Board, "Description of Components," https://www.conference-board.org/data/bci/index.cfm?id=2160

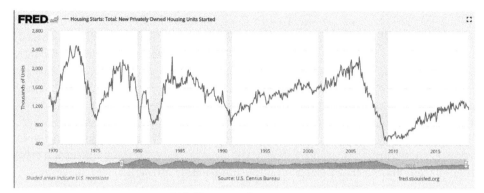

9.10: US Housing Starts, 1970–2018

The Federal Reserve calculates its own leading index for the US economy by examining unemployment, manufacturing, the interest rate spread between the 10-year Treasury bond and the three-month Treasury bill, and housing starts, as seen in figure 9.11.

Figure 9.11: US Leading Index, 1982–2018

9.2   Cycle *Times*

A common source of frustration for analysts, policymakers, and academics alike is predicting the *duration* of a business cycle. No one has an exact answer to "How long will it take for the economy to recover from recession?" All we can do, is look to how long it took for the economy to recover from previous recessions.

Table 9.1 shows data on the 33 business cycles that the US has experienced over a 155-year period. Beginning in the fourth quarter of 1854 the table shows the number of months that each of the US economy's business cycles lasted. Also, at the bottom of the table, we see that since 1854 contractions have gotten shorter and expansions have gotten longer. Overall, US business cycles have gotten longer, 48.9 to 68.5 months.

Table 9.1: US Business Cycle Expansions and Contractions[7]

BUSINESS CYCLE REFERENCE DATES		DURATION IN MONTHS			
Peak	Trough	Contraction	Expansion	Cycle	
Quarterly dates are in parentheses		Peak to Trough	Previous trough to this peak	Trough from Previous Trough	Peak from Previous Peak
	December 1854 (IV)	--	--	--	--
June 1857(II)	December 1858 (IV)	18	30	48	--
October 1860(III)	June 1861 (III)	8	22	30	40
April 1865(I)	December 1867 (I)	32	46	78	54
June 1869(II)	December 1870 (IV)	18	18	36	50
October 1873(III)	March 1879 (I)	65	34	99	52
March 1882(I)	May 1885 (II)	38	36	74	101
March 1887(I)	April 1888 (I)	13	22	35	60
July 1890(III)	May 1891 (II)	10	27	37	40
January 1893(I)	June 1894 (II)	17	20	37	30
December 1895(IV)	June 1897 (II)	18	18	36	35
June 1899(III)	December 1900 (IV)	18	24	42	42
September 1902(IV)	August 1904 (III)	23	21	44	39
May 1907(II)	June 1908 (II)	13	33	46	56
January 1910(I)	January 1912 (IV)	24	19	43	32
January 1913(I)	December 1914 (IV)	23	12	35	36
August 1918(III)	March 1919 (I)	7	44	51	67
January 1920(I)	July 1921 (III)	18	10	28	17
May 1923(II)	July 1924 (III)	14	22	36	40
October 1926(III)	November 1927 (IV)	13	27	40	41
August 1929(III)	March 1933 (I)	43	21	64	34
May 1937(II)	June 1938 (II)	13	50	63	93
February 1945(I)	October 1945 (IV)	8	80	88	93
November 1948(IV)	October 1949 (IV)	11	37	48	45
July 1953(II)	May 1954 (II)	10	45	55	56
August 1957(III)	April 1958 (II)	8	39	47	49
April 1960(II)	February 1961 (I)	10	24	34	32
December 1969(IV)	November 1970 (IV)	11	106	117	116
November 1973(IV)	March 1975 (I)	16	36	52	47
January 1980(I)	July 1980 (III)	6	58	64	74
July 1981(III)	November 1982 (IV)	16	12	28	18
July 1990(III)	March 1991(I)	8	92	100	108
March 2001(I)	November 2001 (IV)	8	120	128	128
December 2007 (IV)	June 2009 (II)	18	73	91	81
Average, all cycles:					
1854-2009 (33 cycles)		17.5	38.7	56.2	56.4*
1854-1919 (16 cycles)		21.6	26.6	48.2	48.9**
1919-1945 (6 cycles)		18.2	35.0	53.2	53.0
1945-2009 (11 cycles)		11.1	58.4	69.5	68.5

* 32 cycles
** 15 cycles

---

[7]National Bureau of Economic Research, "US Business Cycle Expansions and Contractions," https://www.nber.org/cycles/

9.3   Real Business Cycles

Followers of *real business cycle* theory believe that aggregate economic activity is the result of macroeconomic decisions, like the individual utility and maximization choices of individual consumers and firms. When faced with a *shock*, we ask how and in what way, *individual* laborers, firms, and consumers will respond, over the length of adjustment.

As we discussed in chapter 7, according to classical theory, in the long-run, the economy will reach a state of full employment; however, in the short-run, demand and supply shocks prevent markets from maintaining equilibrium. If the economy experiences an adverse demand shock, causing $Y_t < Y^*$, no action needs be taken by the government or the central bank; since the economy is *self-correcting*, price levels will adjust quickly and long-run equilibrium will be restored. If there *is* any intervention on the part of the government, all it will accomplish is distorting the market, possibly worsening the recession. What concerns followers of real business cycle theory is not shocks to AD, since price levels are expected to adjust quickly to correct the market, but shocks to AS.

Any exogenous change in productivity or the supply of labor affects the production function. These *productivity shocks* affect the position of the $LRAS$ curve. If the economy experiences a positive productivity shock, $LRAS$ shifts to the right and the economy experiences *expansion*. Any negative productivity shock such that we see a reduction in the full-employment level of GDP will shift the $LRAS$ to the right, causing *recession*.

9.3.1   Policy under Real Business Cycles

Followers of real business cycle theory feel that neither fiscal nor monetary policy have any *real* effect on improving economic performance. Monetary policy only fights against price stability, and fiscal policy only improves economic conditions by changing taxes, which undermines the functioning of the market.

RBC proponents suggest minimal money growth, to stabilize price levels, keeping inflation low, and caution against the use of tax policy to affect changes in spending due to the distortive nature of taxes.

9.3.2   Criticism

Real business cycle theory has been called into question based on a few points:

- Assumption of Full Employment

Real business cycle theory assumes that the economy is always at full-employment. In order for this to be true, two things must be true. First, both wages and prices must adjust quickly to changes in the market; also, any short-run fluctuation in output represents a movement of the full-employment level of output.

- Assumption of Technology

The theory is based on the assumption that the *only* shocks that have a real effect are technological shocks. The existence of technological shocks is often called into question. In his 1986 paper, Lawrence Summers notes that there is no "corroborating evidence for the existence of . . . *technological shocks.*" Summers states that the RBC literature offers "no discussion of the source or nature of these shocks, nor . . . any microeconomic evidence for their importance."[8]

Putting that aside, technological change, when it happens, only affects the specific industry in which it occurs. It is hard to see technology having an economy-wide effect. Additionally, any change that does occur is expected to experience a *lag* effect. Given this lag, how could technological shocks have a *short-run* effect?

- Assumption of Policy Ineffectiveness

The theory assumes that monetary policy is ineffective in influencing wage and price level changes, since they are quick to adjust to shocks. Realistically, we have seen real-world evidence that wages and prices do not adjust as quickly in the short run, and *some* policy measures are needed to restore equilibrium.

- Lucas Critique

Some economists have called into question the validity of using historical macroeconomic data alone as a tool for measuring economic performance, on which policy recommendations can be made. In his 1976 paper,[9] Robert Lucas spoke on the dangers of ignoring the *micro-foundations* of the macroeconomy. Rather than looking at the economy, as a whole, the focus of macroeconomic inquiry should be on the parameters that govern the behavior of *individual* firms, laborers, and consumers. Only after the individual has been considered, can the individual behaviors be aggregated to find the macroeconomic effects on the market.

---

[8]Lawrence H. Summers. "Some Skeptical Observations on Real Business Cycle Theory," *Federal Reserve Bank of Minneapolis Quarterly Review* 10, no. 4 (Fall 1986): 23–27.

[9]Robert Lucas, "Econometric Policy Evaluation: A Critique". *The Phillips Curve and Labor Markets*, eds. Karl Brunner and Allan Meltzer (New York: American Elsevier, 1976), 19–46.

9.4   Alternative Theories

There are multiple *other* theories that seek to explain economic fluctuations. We will now examine a few.

9.4.1   Keynesian Business Cycle

Followers of Keynesian theory believe that shocks to *IS/LM*, which cause aggregate demand shifts, are the cause of business cycle fluctuation. These shocks, as we discussed in chapter 7, include both fiscal and monetary policy, changes in the expectations about future productivity, as well as changes in consumer confidence. Changes to aggregate demand drive the economy. When *AD* is high, spending and income are high. Firms respond to increases in demand by increasing production, which results in the increased of employment and income level. If aggregate demand is low, the opposite is true.

According to Keynesian business cycle theory, recessions are caused by negative shocks to *AD*. While it is true that Keynesians believe that the market will recover *eventually*, with price levels adjusting to bring the market to its long-run equilibrium, it is felt that in such a case, expansionary fiscal and/or monetary policy should be utilized to equilibriate the market. Intervention, however, is inflationary. Price levels tend to rise, as a result of expansionary policies, while, in the absence of intervention, the market would have equilibriated at a lower price level.

■ Criticism

To discuss the efficacy of utilizing policy in order to stabilize the economy, we must consider the existence of *lags*. There are five kinds of lags that policy implementation face:

1. Information lag
   Data on the current state of the economy is not reported daily. In order to record recessive GDP, the economy must first be in a recession. It takes months for the the recession to be recorded, a period during which, the economy is already suffering.

2. Recognition lag
   After the data has been recorded, it must be interpreted by an analyst. Recognizing the recession is dependent on the analysts skill.

3. Legislation lag
   After the analyst has reported the existence of the recession, for which the economy requires stimulus, a considerable period of time must be spent as policy-makers discuss *specifically* what policy should be utilized.

4. Implementation lag
   Once a policy has been agreed to, time is required for the policy to be put
   into effect.

5. Effectiveness lag
   After the policy has been implemented, time is required for the policy to
   effect change in the economy. This can range anywhere from months to
   years.

Given the lag effects, and in the interest of not distorting the economy, policy
should only be used to fix extreme disequilibria, not smooth out small fluctuations.

9.4.2 Austrian Business Cycle

Followers of Ludwig von Mises and Friedrich Hayek believe that business cycles
are driven by central bank policies. Low interest rates incentivize borrowing. As
more borrowing is used to finance increases in spending, the economy *appears* to
be prosperous. This, in fact, is not prosperity, but rather a speculative bubble.
At some point, interest rates will increase, bringing an end to the borrowing and
causing the economy to recess.

Under such cycles, the fiscal and monetary policies only extend unsustainable
market conditions. Since the market is driven by borrowing, a banking system
based on *fractional-reserves* is quite dangerous, and the only way to avoid problems, is through the elimination and avoidance of debt.

■ Criticism

If the Austrian theory is correct, bankers and borrowers continually make illogical
decisions, not in the best interest of themselves or the market.

9.4.3 Goodwin Model

First proposed by Richard Goodwin, in 1967, the model[10] ignores exogenous
shocks and instead focuses on the effect employment has on wages and profit.
In periods of prosperity, unemployment is low. In periods of low unemployment,
it is assumed there will be upward pressure on wages. If wages increase enough,
firms will see significant reductions in profit, which de-incentivizes investment and
therefore, production. As investment and production decrease, demand for labor
decreases, which will lead to decreases in wages. This will lead to increases in the
firm's profits, which leads to increases investment and production, necessitating
increases in labor demand.

---

[10]Richard M. Goodwin, "A Growth Cycle," *Socialism, Capitalism and Economic Growth*
(Cambridge, MA: Cambridge University Press, 1967), 165-170, ed. C. H. Feinstein.

Food for Thought

1. What is the current level of US inflation?

2. What is the current level of US unemployment?

3. Given the answers to 2 and 3, what stage of the business cycle is the US currently in?

   - Answer the same question for the European Union

   - Peru?

   - South Africa?

Chapter 10

Unemployment and Inflation

> We're all trying to experiment to
> find a way to live, to solve
> problems, to fend off madness and
> chaos.
>
> David Cronenberg

As we have seen throughout this book, economies tend to work, unless price levels or unemployment become problematic. It is also believed that a negative relationship exists between inflation and unemployment, which, if true, means that, given effective fiscal and monetary tools, policymakers have the ability to choose the combination of inflation and unemployment that best suits the economy.

We begin this chapter by looking at the origins of that belief and then consider its larger implications for an economy's future.

10.1   The Phillips Curve

In his 1958 article, William Phillips[1] showed evidence of an inverse empirical relationship between unemployment and wages for the United Kingdom. Two year's later Paul Samuelson and Robert Solow updated Phillips' thesis to show evidence of an inverse relationship between unanticipated inflation and cyclical unemployment.[2]

$$\pi_t - E_{t-1}\pi_t = -\eta(u_t - u^n)$$

where η measures the economy's sensitivity to cyclical unemployment.

Figure 10.1 shows the Phillips curve for which $\pi_t = E_{t-1}\pi_t$ and $u_t = u^n$. Any change in π_t or u_t will result in a movement along the curve.

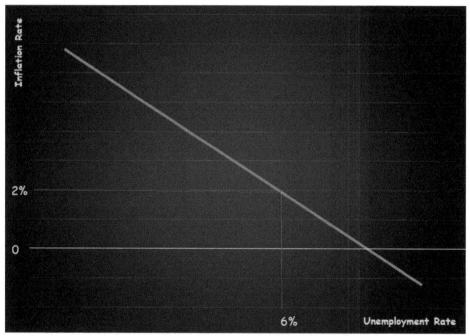

Figure 10.1: The Phillips curve

This *expectations-augmented Phillips curve* states that the only determining factor of cyclical unemployment, is unexpected inflation. As long as changes to the money supply are expected, the economy will remain at full employment. If the

---

[1]William Phillips, "The Relation between Unemployment and the Rate of Change of Money Wage Rates in the United Kingdom 1861-1957," *Economica*, 25, no. 100 (1968): 283-299.

[2]Paul A. Samuelson & Robert M. Solow, "Analytical Aspects of Anti-Inflation Policy," *American Economic Review*, 50, no. 2 (1960): 177-194.

money supply is growing *faster* than anticipated, unemployment will be *below* its natural rate. Likewise, if money growth is *slower* than anticipated, unemployment will be *above* its natural rate. Let us assume that $E_{t-1}\pi_t = 2$ percent and $u^n = 6$ percent.

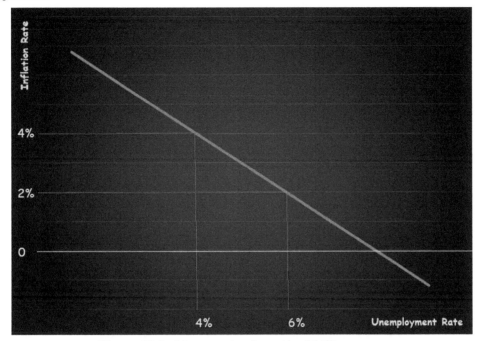

Figure 10.2: Movements along the Phillips curve

As seen in figure 10.2, if inflation is *above* the expected rate, unemployment will fall below its natural rate natural rate.

$$\pi_t = E_{t-1}\pi_t \quad u_t = u^n \quad \text{Full employment}$$
$$\pi_t > E_{t-1}\pi_t \quad u_t < u^n \quad \text{Inflationary GDP}$$
$$\pi_t < E_{t-1}\pi_t \quad u_t > u^n \quad \text{Recessionary GDP}$$

10.1.1   Shifting the Phillips Curve

If the Phillips curve is to be believed, the only shifts in the curve occur when there is a change to either $E_{t-1}\pi_t$ or u^n. For any given expected rate of inflation, we know what unemployment will be; however, if expectations change, say, an increase in expected inflation, we see the Phillips curve shift to maintain the level of the natural rate of unemployment.

As seen in figure 10.3, assuming the natural rate of unemployment remains 6 percent, a doubling of expected inflation puts the economy on a higher Phillips curve.

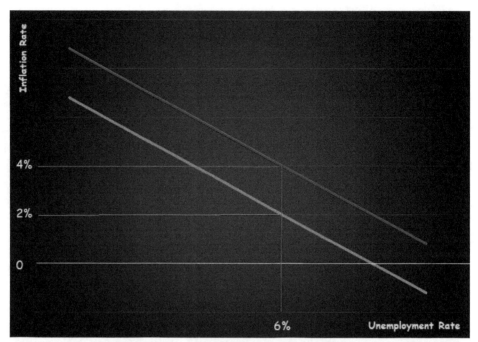

Figure 10.3: Change in expected inflation

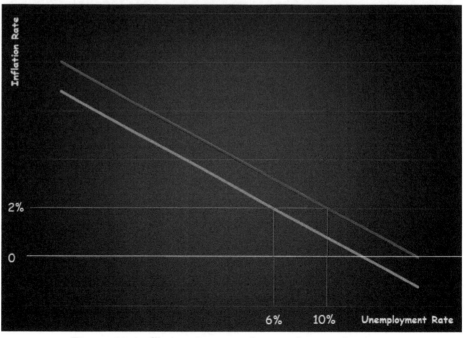

Figure 10.4: Change in natural rate of unemployment

If, instead, there is an increase in the natural rate of unemployment, it will shift the Phillips curve to the right. As seen in figure 10.4, assuming expected inflation remains 2 percent, if the natural rate of unemployment increases to 10 percent, the curve shifts right.

Assuming expected inflation and the natural rate of unemployment remain constant, the Phillips curve tends to be effective. If *both* $E\pi$ and u^n are changing, the curve becomes unstable.

10.1.2   The Long-Run Phillips Curve

In the long run, it is assumed that the economy will be at full employment. This means that unemployment will be at its natural rate *regardless* of the level of inflation. If this is true, the long-run Phillips curve is a vertical line, as seen in Figure 10.5. The perfect inelasticity of the long-run Phillips curve supports the belief that money is neutral, since, in the long-run, increasing the supply of money does not affect the natural rate of unemployment; it only creates inflation.

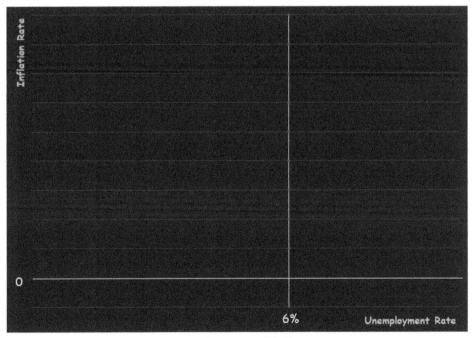

Figure 10.5: Long-run Phillips curve

10.2   Unemployment

As a reminder, unemployment is a measure of the percentage of the labor force that is jobless. The most commonly cited measure of unemployment is U3, which estimates the number of people who are actively seeking a job. When U3 is *above* the natural rate of unemployment, the economy is said to be operating below *full-employment.*

10.2.1   The Natural Rate of Unemployment

We cannot, at any given time, know what the natural rate of unemployment is. Some economists[3] do not believe it can be measured with any accuracy. The difficulty that analysts have measuring the natural rate makes setting policy difficult. Given that policy is set based on estimations of where the economy *would* be if at full-unemployment, it is best that policy-makers take care.

Figure 10.6 shows the natural rate of unemployment reported by the US Congressional Budget Office. In the figure, we see that, since the mid-1970s, u^n has decreased. This may be due to the fact that, with the rise in information technology, job finding has become easier.

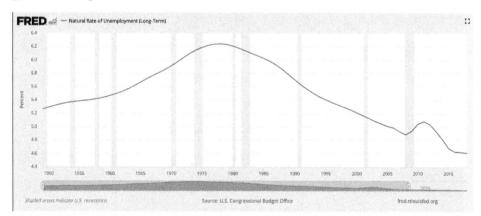

Figure 10.6: Natural rate of unemployment

10.2.2   Okun's Law

Clearly, unemployment poses a microeconomic problem. When laborers are unemployed, they lack the necessary income to be effective consumers, which, if carried to its inevitable conclusion, leads to death (no money = no food).

---

[3]Douglas O. Staiger, James H. Stock, and Mark W. Watson, "How Precise Are Estimates of the Natural Rate of Unemployment?" https://www.nber.org/chapters/c8885

We briefly discussed the macroeconomic problem posed by unemployment in chapter 3. Okun's law illustrates the relationship between unemployment and the full-employment level of GDP. According to Okun, the growth rate of real GDP will be equal to the growth rate of potential GDP so long as there is no change in unemployment. For every 1 percent increase in unemployment, real GDP growth falls by ω percent.

$$\frac{\Delta Y}{Y} = \frac{\Delta Y*}{Y*} - \omega \Delta U_t$$

Using data from the Federal Reserve Bank of St. Louis, regression analysis can be used to estimate the parameters of Okun's law. Regressing quarterly data on the percent change in real GDP and the change in unemployment,

$$\frac{\Delta Y}{Y} = \alpha + \beta(\Delta U_t)$$

where α is the growth rate of potential GDP and β is the effect that changes in unemployment are expected to have on GDP.

Using quarterly data for 1949 through 2018, we find a negative relationship exists between changes in unemployment and the growth rate of GDP. From the regression we see that between 1949 and 2018 the estimated growth rate of potential GDP is 3.2 percent and the Okun coefficient is -1.8, supporting Okun's law.

$$\frac{\Delta Y}{Y} = 3.2 - 1.8\Delta U_t$$

Unemployment is problematic since, its presence makes the economy function suboptimally.

10.2.3   Hysteresis

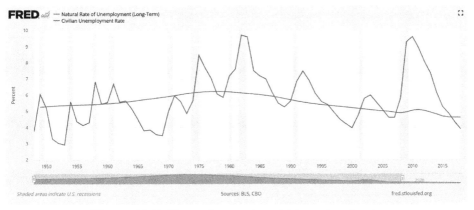

Figure 10.7: Unemployment and the natural rate

Hysteresis occurs when the natural rate of unemployment increases due to increases in the current rate of unemployment. If hysteresis is true, a laborer who becomes unemployed may *never* be employable, in the future. Economists believe that, if workers become unemployed in a recession, and remain so long enough, their human capital deteriorates, making it harder for them to find work when the market recovers.

This, if true, presents a problem for policymakers. In the absence of hysteresis, any unemployment that results from inflation-fighting contractionary policy will disappear in the long run. In the presence of hysteresis, the unemployment caused by the policy will permanently increase the natural rate of unemployment, and the unemployed will remain so.

10.3   Inflation

Inflation is the measure of the rate at which the average price level is increasing. When unanticipated, inflation adversely affects the purchasing power of a nation's currency.

10.3.1   Anticipated Inflation

Figure 10.8 shows US expectation of inflation for 1978–2018.

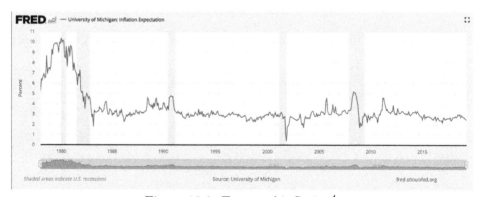

Figure 10.8: Expected inflation[4]

As we discussed in chapter 6, inflation poses no true threat, as long as it is anticipated. When inflation is anticipated, both consumers and firms are inconvenienced; however, the shoe leather and menu costs are more of an annoyance than a threat. When inflation is anticipated, laborers know to negotiate increases in

---

[4]Federal Reserve Bank of St. Louis, "University of Michigan: Inflation Expectation," https://fred.stlouisfed.org/series/MICH/

nominal wages, and firms know to raise relative prices. Given that people have *rational expectations*,[5] the social costs of inflation, previously discussed, will be minimal.

10.3.2   Unanticipated Inflation

As we discussed, briefly, in chapter 6, when inflation is unanticipated, the social costs can be quite higher.

■ Price Distortion Effect

On a microeconomic level, consumers and firms use prices to signal preferences. What quantity of a good are consumers willing to buy at a specific price? What quantity are firms willing to produce? Economists use prices to measure how markets are functioning. If we see persistent surpluses or shortages in a market, we know that prices are *too high* or *too low*, and we can predict price movements and changes to consumer and production choices. If prices are distorted (preventing the market from clearing), it undermines their effectiveness as a signal, which is confusing and inconvenient to analysts.

■ Purchasing Power Effect

The rate of return *realized* by an investor (or lender) is affected by whether *actual* inflation is higher or lower than expected. Remember, investing (and lending) is done based on the *ex-ante* real interest rate, which is dependent on *expected* inflation; the actual real interest rate is the *ex-post* real interest rate.

$$
\begin{aligned}
Er_t &= i_t - E_{t-1}\pi_t \\
r_t &= i_t - \pi_t
\end{aligned}
$$

Depending on whether actual inflation ends-up being above or below the expected level of inflation, the nominal value of money borrowed/lent changes, meaning that the value of the money, at the time of repayment, will be different from the value of the money at the time it was borrowed.

State of π	Value	Advantage
$\pi_t < E_{t-1}\pi_t$	$(i_t - E\pi_t) > (i_t - \pi_t)$	Lender
$\pi_t > E_{t-1}\pi_t$	$(i_t - E\pi_t) < (i_t - \pi_t)$	Borrower

If actual inflation is less than expected, the value of the money paid back is *greater* than the value of the money borrowed, transferring purchasing power from the borrower to the lender. Alternatively, if expected inflation is less than actual inflation, purchasing power is transferred from the lender to the borrower.

---

[5]They use all relevant information in forming expectations of economic conditions.

■ Wages and Income

We see a similar effect when it comes to labor contracts. If laborers and firms negotiate wage increases based on expected inflation, they face the same purchasing power transfer problem.

Beautiful Story:
If a labor contract is negotiated such that wages will increase by 2 percent a year, to account for expected inflation, but inflation is *actually* 4 percent, labor's purchasing power is decreasing. Despite the increase in their nominal wage, labor's cost of living is increasing faster than the wage.

To this end, investors, lenders, borrowers, firms, and laborers spend resources in an effort to improve their ability to forecast inflation. Figure 10.9 shows expected inflation, as measured by a survey of consumers, conducted by the University of Michigan, versus core inflation for the years 1978–2018. Here, we see that expectations seem to *trend* with inflation but not accurately *predict* it.

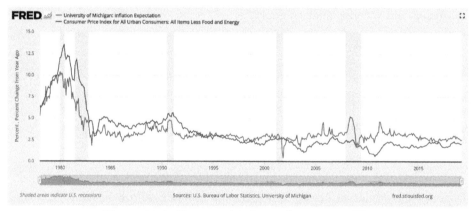

Figure 10.9: Expected inflation[6] vs. core CPI

10.3.3   Dealing with Inflation

■ Cost of Living Adjustments

Indexing contracts to avoid the risk the purchasing power problem poses is common. One option that could be utilized is the use of a cost-of-living adjustment (COLA.) Cost-of-living adjustments index income to the cost of living. They are seen used for wages, contracts, and even Social Security.

---

[6]Ibid.

■ Disinflation

Once inflation has occurred, the central bank can choose to attempt to decrease inflation by reducing the growth rate of money. Classical economists, as we have discussed, believe that a reduction of money growth, through contractionary monetary policy, will cure inflation. Given the assumption that prices adjust quickly, inflation expectations will fall quickly as well.

Given the existence of price stickiness, Keynesians believe that sudden contractionary policy will only lead to recession. For this reason, they recommend the gradual reduction of the money growth rate, over an extended period of time. Since prices fall slowly, inflation expectations will fall slowly as well.

■ Sacrifice Ratio

Given what we know about the Phillips curve and Okun's law, in order to reduce inflation, we expect unemployment to increase, an increase which will lead to a decrease in GDP. The *sacrifice ratio* is the loss in output that is necessary to decrease inflation. In this way, the sacrifice ratio can be considered the *cost* of fighting inflation. Developed by Laurence Ball,[7] the ratio is measured by dividing the loss in GDP (due to recession) by the decrease in inflation.

In his paper, Ball measures the sacrifice ratio for a sample of countries who experienced disinflation between 1961 and 1988, finding that most nations must give up between 1 percent and 3 percent of a year's GDP to reduce inflation by 1 percent. The key, Ball finds, to a less painful disinflation is that the nation's disinflationary policies be quick, not gradual, and the labor market be dynamic and flexible.

---

[7]Ball, Laurence M., What Determines the Sacrifice Ratio? (March 1993). NBER Working Paper No. w4306

Food for Thought

1. Construct and analyze the Phillips curve.
   - Step 1.   Go to the Bureau of Labor Statistics website and find and download historical unemployment data for the US from 1948 to the present.
   - Step 2.   Locate and download CPI data for the US for the same time period.
   - Step 3.   Using these two data series, plot the Phillips curve for 1960–1969, with unemployment on the horizontal and CPI on the vertical axis.
   - Step 4.   Does the graph support what you have learned about the Phillips curve, in this chapter?

     On separate graphs, construct Phillips curves for the 1970s, 1980s, and 2000s.

     How do the subsequent graphs compare to the original? Explain your result.

2. Read *Inflation and the Gig Economy* by John V. Duca.[8] What effect has self-employment had on the Phillips curve?

   ■ How has online shopping affected the natural rate of unemployment?

3. Find a data source for an economic forecast; here[9] is an example. Once you have located your own, read it.
   Does it make sense? Do you agree with it? Why or why not?

You are now a macroeconomist.[10]

---

[8]John V. Duca, "Inflation and the Gig Economy: Have the Rise of Online Retailing and Self-Employment Disrupted the Philip's Curve?" Federal Reserve Bank of Dallas, 2018, https://www.dallasfed.org/-/media/documents/research/papers/2018/wp1814.pdf

[9]"US Economic Outlook: For 2019 and Beyond," *The Balance*, https://www.thebalance.com/us-economic-outlook-3305669

[10]*Let joy be unconfined. Let there be dancing in the streets, drinking in the saloons and necking in the parlor.* -Groucho Marx

Index

CPSIA information can be obtained
at www.ICGtesting.com
Printed in the USA
LVHW061936301221
707564LV00001B/10

9 781516 582228